The New Waterfront

The New Waterfront

A Worldwide Urban Success Story

Ann Breen

and Dick Rigby

with 363 illustrations 177 in colour

Thames and Hudson

We dedicate this book to the hundreds of wonderful, supportive people we've met around the world while pursuing our research, and, especially, to The Most Loyal Order of River Rats.

PREVIOUS PAGES: **A view across the Rhine of the Museum Ludwig and Köln (Cologne) Philharmonic (see p. 211), center left, a dramatic riverfront presence since 1986, with the famed cathedral behind it.**

British Library Cataloguing-in-Publication Data

A catalogue record for this book is available from the British Library

ISBN 500 34145 1

Printed and bound in Singapore by C.S. Graphics Pte Ltd

CONTENTS

PREFACE

We would like to provide a word of explanation about how projects were selected for inclusion in *The New Waterfront*. By definition we consider the bay, canal, lake, pond and river, including the man-made, under the generic term "waterfront." Having spent the last fifteen years (Ann actually dates her urban waterfront research to 1975) tracking waterfront planning and development—largely in North America—we still found the extent and array of recent urban waterfront projects around the globe to be something of a surprise. We know with assurance, however, that there is a great deal more waterfront work being done than even we uncovered. Research for the book began in early 1994, and in the course of developing the final list of projects we identified as many as three hundred candidates. While considerable, this number is surely but a fraction of the total.

Beyond our research files, calls to our circle of friends—which is, happily, increasingly international—and press releases sent to over six hundred outlets, we relied on a search of architectural and related periodicals to identify potential projects. ("Waterfront" is a classification that can be used to search the computer files of domestic and international publications housed at the American Institute of Architects Library.) We made a concerted effort to visit as many works included here as possible within the limits of time and budget. Naturally, this permitted the accidental find. For instance, we journeyed to Helsinki to see two projects, Finlandia Hall and the Helsinki National Opera. While situated close to the banks of Lake Toolonlahti Toloviken, both showed a disappointing lack of water orientation, Finlandia Hall completely so. However, an inquiry at the tourist office led us to Ruoholahti, an ambitious new housing precinct on old harbor lands that we are happy to feature in these pages (see pp. 126–9). In addition to our own inspections, we have relied on those of trusted colleagues and on the recommendations of reliable sources. Of the 130 cases finally included in *The New Waterfront*, we have personally visited over one hundred.

Inevitably it will be asked why a particular project is not included. One reason could be that we visited it and did not feel it measured up: as with Finlandia Hall mentioned above; or Waterstad in Rotterdam (inadequate public space in our minds, and some positively weird architecture); or the Sea Fort Square project in Tokyo (basically an office project with an isolated promenade on the water). It is also possible that we identified a project as promising but were unable to gain cooperation (as in a nicely designed and situated small cafe in Amsterdam). In some cases we were simply unable to reach a contact person.

We focus on built work only. A project needed to be substantially completed or well under construction by the end of 1995. Thus, Il Parco San Giuliano near Venice, Italy, scheduled for completion in 1996, is not included. Likewise, Water Park in Bremerhaven looks interesting but is unbuilt and thus not featured here. In the case of Parc André-Citroën in Paris, it is a stunning installation that is not included because, as of October 1995, it had not made the planned connection to the Seine; when it does, it will be a great waterfront park.

The current urban waterfront phenomenon dates generally from the early 1960s. For a time frame, therefore, we kept to projects of the last thirty years or so. We have been deliberately imprecise here, allowing ourselves to include the classic Paseo del Rio in San Antonio, whose resuscitation dates from the early 1960s, and the moving Paris memorial to French victims of the Holocaust, 1962.

We consciously sought and selected a variety of projects in an effort to document the fact that today's urban waterfront is home to myriad enterprises, that cultural and public-realm undertakings are as prevalent, or more so, than the better-publicized commercial projects, and that there is room for industry as well as for housing and for all in between. Thus, we have thirty entries in the cultural/educational/environmental category, and twenty-five commercial works. In addition to showing a variety of types of projects, we include schemes from small as well as large cities, underscoring the point that waterfront regeneration is happening in places of all sizes. Therefore, we have Husum in northern Germany, Zushi, south of Yokohama in Japan, and Strahan, population five hundred, in Tasmania, Australia. Inevitably it is the larger design firms working in larger cities that are most publicized; knowing this, we sought a counterbalance. We also looked for projects in developing countries, as well as in Eastern Europe and in the Arab Gulf, but have to confess to a general lack of success in establishing fruitful contacts in these areas.

Because of the range of geography, population and types of waterfront projects, it should be obvious that there can be no single set of criteria by which one project is included, another not. Philosophically we are opposed to formulas. Instead, we looked at each work individually, noting, for instance, such characteristics as the amount of public access at the water's edge, the civic contribution, and the "fit" of the project in scale, material and style, be it bold, modern or an adaptive reuse of a former warehouse. Such a subjective approach will no doubt disappoint those who are interested in developing "models" and lists of five, seven or ten essential elements that constitute successful waterfront projects. We hope the range of waterfront developments illustrated here will dispel the notion that any set number of characteristics could meaningfully cover work in, for example, Antwerp, as well as in Boston, Cape Town, Kobe and Whangarei.

We provide data and contacts for each project for the reader to use. The data is gleaned from questionnaires filled out by individuals involved and from published literature. In some cases, particularly on cost, many were reluctant to supply figures. The chapter assignment of projects is sometimes arbitrary. Navy Pier in Chicago we place with commercial projects, but it could be called historic as well. Likewise, Castlefield in Manchester, UK, is with historic projects and could as well be included in recreation or commercial. The groupings are a convenience and our placement reflects the outstanding or dominant characteristic we see. Civic undertakings, such as city hall in Husum, we classify with commercial schemes.

A word or two on what we have *not* attempted to cover in this account, namely waterfront resorts and the related subject of spas. Generally speaking, places like Port Grimaud, France; Costa Smeralda, Sardinia; Sea Ranch, California; Seaside, Florida, and Harbor Town, South Carolina, are specialty vacation destinations, second-home resorts and escapes, and are not urban waterfronts in the sense and spirit that we use the term for in this book. In our view, these places are often quite exclusive and private, and already much written about.

A final note. We like to think that the popular success of many new waterfronts is a tangible sign of the vitality of cities, even in a world increasingly dominated by suburbs. That the inherent magic of water will draw people together at certain places or for special events is proof that the growing sense of isolation in our cities does not have to be.

We welcome reader comments and suggestions of other works. We can be reached in care of The Waterfront Center, 1622 Wisconsin Avenue NW, Washington, D.C. 20007 USA; fax 1 202 625 1654.

A.B./D.R.

INTRODUCTION

Background on the Worldwide Urban Waterfront Phenomenon

This book concerns itself with the area where cities engage their shorelines—the urban waterfront. The very fabric of many cities around the world is inextricably linked to the bodies of water that contributed to their founding and to their subsequent development. Some of the planet's most fascinating cities— Hamburg and Rotterdam, Sydney and Hong Kong, Rio de Janeiro and Cape Town, New York and Tokyo — are famous mainly for their waterfront character. The new story that we try to capture here is of the redevelopment that has been taking place in these and lesser-known areas during the last thirty years or so.

The first point to make is that the waterfront regeneration phenomenon is widespread, occurring in thousands of communities in all parts of the globe. If we consider urban waterfront development since about 1965 on every type of water body, and count projects of all types and scale, we are looking at possibly several thousand cities and towns in the US and Canada alone, hundreds of case examples each in the UK and Japan, and scores of projects throughout Europe, Australia, New Zealand and Asia. There is no way to obtain a precise number for these developments, even if tight definitions are agreed to—the occurrence is simply too pervasive and complex.

Within Japan, for example, as of 1993, there were sixty-three documented examples of major waterfront redevelopments involving former port lands either planned or in progress, according to the Waterfront Revitalization Research Center (WARRC). An account by the development firm NIC, which uses finer detail in determining what constitutes a waterfront project, states that there are 107 projects within the Osaka Bay area alone; sixty-five of these have projected costs totaling $120 billion. This effort reflects a dramatic change in the attitude of the Japanese, since the waterfront was previously seen as an area that was strictly for industry, transportation, fishing and flood protection. Now leisure is becoming increasingly important and the process of deindustrialization is opening up vast new territories.

Likewise, in 1989 a survey in the UK found ninety waterfront redevelopment projects under way, seventy of which involved ten acres or more; forty-five were on rivers, twenty-seven along canals, and the balance on bays and harbors. Housing was found to be the major use in thirty schemes.[1]

A second point follows from the first—recent urban waterfront transformations are enormous enterprises, sweeping in scale, and, taken collectively, represent a dramatic story of urban rebirth. If the US and the UK may fairly be said to have taken the lead with early work dating to the late 1950s, other nations, particularly in Asia, are rapidly catching up. In Japan in particular the waterfront projects are of a scale and complexity unlike those found anywhere else.

A SUCCESS STORY—AND THE DARK SIDE

Waterfront redevelopment and expansion is, in short, the best current example globally of the resilience of cities, of their ability to adapt to changed circumstances, to adjust to new technological impacts, to seize opportunities and to forge new images for themselves, as well as to create new or altered neighborhoods for their inhabitants. As we will see, urban waterfront projects do not always succeed. But where they do, they have a dramatic and visible impact that is capable not only of enriching a city's economy but of improving its collective self-image.

There is a quality about water which calls to the most deep-rooted and atavistic part of our nature. In the deep canyons of our cities, water, along with fire, trees and the almost hidden sky above, are the elements which can still tie us to our primitive past. Of all these, water and fire evoke the most direct responses. Fire in the city is dangerous, negative and evil; while water is positive and life-giving — the element from which we all have come. The wildness and exuberance of water stirs us with its qualities of non-conformity and vigor.

Lawrence Halprin, *Cities*, 1963

OPPOSITE: **A pedestrian bridge leading to an island in Tokyo Bay is part of the 100-acre Sea Life Park built on a former landfill (see p. 202).**

BELOW: **Office towers along the Chicago River in downtown Chicago.**

11

**Part of the generous public spaces at Granville
Island, Vancouver, B.C. (see p. 195). The public
market is visible in the background.**

We term this process an "urban success story" because, on the whole, it is. However, that is different from saying every scheme is splendid or a "success," either in economic terms or in design. The real success story to us is the combined effort in the first place, which usually involves some degree of private initiative along with municipal or other governmental intervention—an exercise of community will to make things better. What is important is that cities are doing what they have to in order to remain competitive, and using vacant land near cleaned-up waterways is an obvious step.

Industry, transportation facilities and ports were moved away from central city locations in a trend that has been accelerating since World War II. This huge relocation is the trigger for waterfront regeneration—the departed factory, loading dock or rail yard opened up core city space that was ripe for conversion to other uses, often at low prices and involving little displacement of residential neighborhoods. This phenomenon constitutes a historic shift of resources, comparable to the industrialization of many Western and Asian waterfronts at the turn of the century. Older European cities have also been affected. In Paris, for example, where portions of the Seine riverfront were once devoted to industry and transportation, sites have now been converted to create Le Parc André-Citroën on the western edge, the new National Library on rail yards in the east, and nearby Parc de la Villette along canals where cattle and coal yards once dominated.

However, while the urban waterfront story is positive in general, and a hopeful sign for cities everywhere, it is not without a troubling, or dark, side. The modernization of manufacturing and goods-handling has led to significant job losses in industrialized countries. New waterfront development, however beneficial, by no means constitutes a replacement of the blue-collar jobs that once existed in these areas. The waterfront turnaround then, may be seen as a success story with an underlying consequence that constitutes one of today's most fundamental social problems in developed countries—lack of job prospects for unskilled workers. There is also the related issue of gentrification. In some cases resident neighborhoods

of predominantly poor people have not been well served in the name of waterfront development. Communities in Tiger Bay in Cardiff, the Isle of Dogs in London and along the river in Singapore have been ignored, relocated, or worse, as new, more affluent, populations move in.

ABOVE: **Every hour a fountain spray arches over the Chicago River where it meets Lake Michigan.**

That said, there is a good deal of commentary about "authenticity" or the lack of it along today's waterfront that is idle romanticism. Typical travel accounts relish only the colorful fishing fleets and similar industry on the waterfront and are disdainful of the rest. These critics are not dealing with the reality of abandoned factories and power plants, rotted piers and weedy wastelands that constitute many waterfronts. Vast stretches of decaying waterfront property left behind by relocated industry and ports or by defunct fishing fleets now demand new uses if their cities are to be viable. The trick is to retain as much of the original industrial character as possible (see Granville Island, Vancouver, B.C., in the Gazetteer, p.195).

BELOW: **A handsome new beachfront at Fort Lauderdale, Florida, replaces a car park (see p. 190).**

13

BASIC CONSIDERATIONS

In the classic phrase of American anthropologist Loren Eiseley, "If there is magic on this planet, it is contained in water." Water is a fundamental attraction in all cultures and among all classes of people, from Alaska to Angola to Argentina. It is a favorite location for celebrations and ceremonies, for evening picnics on the beaches of Bahrain, religious rites on the Ganges River in Benares, for dragon boat races in Shanghai, and for New Year's oceanfront offerings for the goddess Eimanja in Brazil. Whether for ritual or recreation, people seek the water's edge. The town of Santos, Brazil, provides a poignant example of this primeval urge (see p. 194). The beaches there, even at their most polluted, drew busloads of weekend visitors from the crowded streets and slums of São Paulo, so strong was the draw of the water.

Magic and poetry aside, water was the *raison d'être* for man's earliest settlements, as a necessary source of nourishment, irrigation and transportation. The ancient inhabitants of Egypt who lived along the Nile, those who settled London on the Thames and Rome on the Tiber, the colonists who founded Sydney on the banks of Botany Bay and the pioneers who founded Chicago at the junction of the river and Lake Michigan are proof that the city by water is a constant throughout history. A vital part of the record of civilization involves events and developments that have occurred along the world's coasts, rivers, bays and lakes; we're tackling here only the most recent chapter. Our focus on the past thirty years or so corre-

14

The storied waterfront of Venice, Italy, with the dome of St. Mark's basilica, which dates from the early seventeenth century.

sponds to the time when many communities began to perceive urban waterfront areas as possible assets, rather than as abandoned, physically deteriorated, problematic tracts on polluted water bodies.

The change in attitude occurred in different places at different times and involved some similar basic factors, but always in response to unique, localized considerations. The earliest stirrings came in London and Liverpool in the UK, and in Oakland, Seattle and San Francisco, in the US, with planning dating to the late 1950s and first building activity to the early '60s. Sydney's spectacular Opera House also dates from this period as does the rebirth of the Paseo del Rio in San Antonio, Texas. These early transformations began a trend that continues today and has spread from North America and England to Australia, Japan and the entire Pacific Rim, to Scandinavia, the Netherlands and throughout Europe. The waterfront movement has also picked up around the globe—in Latin America, the Middle East, South Africa.

One reason the urban waterfront phenomenon has spread so widely in a relatively short time is that, thanks to airplanes, phones and fax machines, more people have had more ready access to all parts of the world and more ways to glean information than at any time previously. Word of the success of early waterfront regeneration projects, particularly in North America and the UK, drew architects, project managers, developers and mayors from around the world to visit and learn firsthand about schemes that work. Conferences, publications and videos informed still more people. An unfortunate result is the rote copying of projects that are perceived to be successes, whether they are appropriate to the new locale or not.

Individual waterfront projects can have a remarkable local and worldwide influence. Baltimore's Inner Harbor transformation is known—or felt to be known—the world over. Surrounding a tiny water body, in a city desperately trying to hang on to its downtown, the thirty-year development of the Inner Harbor from derelict wharves to a multifaceted attraction that draws millions of visitors to the city annually is truly stunning. Countless delegations from all parts of the world have come to Baltimore to learn from its success. Darling Harbour in Sydney, Barcelona's Port Vell and Cardiff Bay, Wales, are some of the places that trace their roots directly to the Inner Harbor. An interesting aside to this is contained in a Japanese compilation entitled *Italian Aquascapes*.[2] Author Hidenobu Jinnai urges Japanese planners to stop visiting large-scale projects in the UK, USA or Australia and instead to absorb the lessons of waterfront cities in Italy:

> *There is surely no longer any need for planners and designers, especially in Japan, to be too concerned about such large-scale developments as the Docklands project in London, nor any need to spend any more time inspecting the waterfront developments which have been carried out in various cities in the United States and Australia.*
>
> *When we start thinking along these lines it is the waterfront areas and spaces in which water plays such an important role to be found all over Italy that really start to be so appealing. They (the cities) have all developed in their own particular way over the years, and their backgrounds are a wealth of enshrined memories and stories. They have all grown and developed over the centuries, they are all of a human scale, and are a pleasure to walk around. They make the best possible use of the topography, and are consequently unique "stages of life" peculiar to their location.*

We agree.

While the globalized, almost instantaneous, availability of project information certainly helped spread the word, a host of factors underlie the current urban waterfront regeneration phenomenon. We will cite some here, with the caveat that every place—each city and town—has its own history, politics and economic role, meaning these generalizations apply only somewhat or not at all to as many cities around the globe as they accurately describe. Also, making blanket statements about developments in such disparate places as Kobe, Japan, Buenos Aires, Argentina, and Mikkeli, Finland, runs an obvious risk.

***Tidal Cascade* is a water sculpture by Robert Woodward set in the promenade at Sydney's Darling Harbour (see pp. 40–3).**

UNDERLYING CAUSES

Waterfront regeneration schemes necessarily involve a variety of economic, social, environmental and preservation issues.

Economic

We are seeing a massive deindustrialization of city centers that began in the most developed countries and is now spreading. This is often the result of changes in technology that cause many ports to relocate away from traditional central sites, a phenomenon that is as true for Amsterdam as it is for London, Singapore and Manama, Bahrain.

Yet, while many commentators focus solely on this change in port technology, an even larger factor is the shift from traditional industrial sites on water. The mills of Lowell in Massachusetts, and Leeds in England, for example, were abandoned long ago. But more recently, even postwar construction has been left behind. Modernized shipyards ceased operations in Philadelphia in autumn 1995. Still more waterfront lands were freed up for development by the decreased need for railroad holdings, which was sometimes related to relocated shipping or industry but otherwise simply reflected the railroads' process of consolidation. This process also involved a fundamental shift of industry from city to suburbs, and from older industrial lands to newer locales (i.e., from Japan to Taiwan, from North America to Mexico, etc.).

Another factor is the bombing of ports and industry during World War II which left a lot of land that required rebuilding in such cities as Berlin, Rotterdam and Yokohama, among many others. The consequence of these changes to the city centers is that vast stretches of territory, often low in price, opened up in cities throughout the world.

Social

Our global culture today desires more open space for recreation and physical activities. With the rise of the middle class and changing labor patterns in many countries, many people enjoy more leisure time. More time and more mobility have caused an expansion of tourism in general, and the emergence of what has come to be called "cultural tourism" and "eco-tourism," each with its own nuances. These related factors add up to a market for sophisticated installations along water bodies that combine areas of open space and leisure with shops, cafes and restaurants, and provide cultural as well as recreational attractions. These establishments cater not only to local residents and the traditional tourist but also to visitors from nearby areas—the regional tourists.

One feature of this general phenomenon, which is readily documented, is the rise in the number of public festivals. We use the rapid growth of the Stockholm Water Festival in this work (see p. 216) to illustrate the relatively recent flourishing of a time-honored activity. The International Festivals Association, an association of worldwide festival organizers, has grown from a membership of two hundred, in 1984, to

**An outdoor cafe, tour boat and hotel are all part of
the famous canal culture that defines Amsterdam.**

approximately 1,300, in 1994. Not surprisingly, festivals are often held on or close to a city's main water-front. The many parks, amphitheaters and other performance venues become focal points for the residents of a city to gather and celebrate and enjoy music, food, literature, dance or maritime heritage.

For better or worse, in developed countries there is an increased emphasis on shopping as entertainment, a fact that is reflected in many mixed-use waterfront projects. The North American recreational "cruise" through the shopping mall is being exported around the globe. Even more common is the interest in dining by the water. Hence, the worldwide proliferation of waterside restaurants, featuring not only seafood but various styles and cuisines that are increasing in popularity and sophistication globally.

ABOVE: **The Chicago lakefront remains largely**

open space, a legacy that dates from the turn

of the century, when development was blocked.

BELOW: **A bold new passenger vessel terminal**

at Naka Pier in Kobe, Japan (see p. 199).

Environmental

Since the 1970s there has been an emphasis, in developed countries especially, on cleaning up bodies of water and water supplies. The demand for water cleanup in the interest of health and, not incidentally, to encourage new waterfront investment is now widely appreciated. There are many dramatic stories of such cleanup schemes around the world. Cleaner water is a crucial factor in most current urban waterfront work. That is to say that until the canals in central Birmingham were cleaned up, little investment, civic or private, was taking place along them. As recently as ten years ago, the canalsides there were a no-man's-land. The dramatic comeback related in these pages (see pp. 52–5) is built on an investment in water purification, a process that has been repeated in countless water cleanup efforts around the world.

Preservation

This is, perhaps, a less obvious influence than water cleanup, but historic preservation and the adaptive reuse of heritage buildings have received increased emphasis in many countries since the 1970s. In large part this is a reaction against the prevalent modern architecture, which has left the public cold, so to speak, and the even worse effects of urban planners and transportation engineers worldwide who mounted concrete assaults on cities in the buildup after World War II. The trend toward cultural tourism has caused more than one city to take a second look at the economic potential inherent in the preservation and restoration of their historic buildings and landscapes. The town of Lowell, Massachusetts, which fought urban renewal clearance in an effort to save its heritage, is now home to a national park and is a major tourist attraction (see p. 191).

It may be said that historic preservation of buildings, per se, is not so much a concern in Japan and other Asian countries, although there are signs of growing interest. The Boat Quay and Clarke Quay in

A busy roadway that once severed Düsseldorf, Germany, from the Rhine River was placed in a tunnel in 1993, making way for a new riverfront parliament structure, center right, and riverfront park and telecommunications tower (see p. 208).

Singapore, for example, involved historic preservation as well as major water cleanup. The conscious effort to retain some of the elements of early Singapore, including the recent revival of the revered Raffles Hotel amid an office-tower boom, represents civic recognition of the fact that tourists want to see something of the city's "character."

What an appreciation for historic preservation has meant in a number of cases is a new way of looking at discarded waterfront structures, though not always with positive results. In London, the earliest waterfront redevelopment effort, at St. Katharine's Dock, resulted in the tearing down of some handsome warehouses.[3] Likewise, attractive warehouse buildings that lined London Dock came down to make way for a newspaper plant. The resulting adverse reaction, however, meant that subsequent developments were more sympathetic; the London Docklands Development Corporation had a declared emphasis on building preservation in the 1980s, even while it spawned massive new construction.

Perhaps the unifying element around the globe, as it relates to recent urban waterfront phenomena, is the public's desire to be near a body of water—a rather sharp contrast to the time when many waterfront areas were lined with heavy industry, docks and fenced-off warehouses, or marred by abandonment and

dereliction. The dramatic transformation of a deteriorated waterfront in Kuching, Sarawak, Malaysia, recounted in these pages (see pp. 148-51), is typical of a city adjusting and adapting to changing economic and cultural circumstances. Today a surge of people come to recreate on the beautiful riverwalk, which has risen from a once-thriving commercial shoreline that had become a squatters' haven.

MAJOR TRANSFORMATIONS

Many projects today are large, and a few such as London's Docklands, at five thousand acres, are truly gigantic in size. Cardiff Bay's proposed regeneration will cover 2,700 acres, two hundred alone on its Inner Harbour. Yokohama's Minato Mirai 21 project covers 460 acres, while the Darling Harbour project in Sydney transformed 148 acres (see pp.40–3).

On a different kind of scale, the Kop van Zuid project in Rotterdam, 308 acres, will link the northern and southern sides of that city, two areas that traditionally have been of different social classes. The addition of a dramatic new bridge is the major symbolic step in uniting the two communities (see p. 215).

There are discernible trends amid all the waterfront development taking place. New aquarium facilities are a growing waterfront phenomenon. The Boston (1969) and Baltimore (1981) aquariums set the pace; Monterey (1984) followed with a different design and program. These facilities have become major influences on the style and content of new aquariums being built worldwide, such as in Osaka (1990) and Taipei (1995). Privately operated facilities have also been opened in Sydney and Barcelona.

Another trend, if this is not too strong a term, is the desire for roadways that do not undermine the appearance of a waterfront. Oslo owes its exciting and popular Aker Brygge project to the basic decision to put a heavily traveled highway through the area in a tunnel. Likewise, Cardiff's waterfront roadway is now in a tunnel. Another roadway, in Düsseldorf, has been similarly enclosed (see the Rhine Embankment Tunnel, p. 208), while Boston is at work on such a scheme and Portland, Oregon, years ago took up its

ABOVE: **The Paseo del Rio in San Antonio, Texas, is one of the earliest waterfront developments in the United States, dating its renaissance to the early 1960s (see p. 193).**

BELOW: **Twin pylons at Nybroviken on the Stockholm waterfront, by Christopher Garney, measure environmental conditions. They were built in 1993 after a competition among students at Stockholm College of Arts, Crafts and Design.**

19

A replica of an old sailing vessel is one of the attractions along the Southbank Riverwalk on the St. John's River. Downtown Jacksonville, Florida, rises up in the distance.

20

waterfront expressway in favor of a park and relocated the traffic to the other side of the river. A recurring corollary theme in this book, in fact, is the ways in which waterfront vehicular traffic is handled.

FAILURES AND FLAWS

Are there waterfront failures and flawed efforts? Yes. Canary Wharf, the centerpiece of the colossal Docklands redevelopment in London, has been a financial and planning disaster. Other parts of the attempted makeover of the Isle of Dogs, where Canary Wharf sits, are troubled, and still other components of the overall Docklands project, as at Surrey Docks, are examples of how not to make new communities.

From our point of view, the biggest mistake at Canary Wharf was the lifting of planning controls, meaning effectively that the project was totally market-driven. In fact, the first chief executive was said to have been against a "grand strategy," preferring what was termed a "project-by-project" approach. Thus, to appeal to the perceived market, remnants of the old Isle of Dogs working-class neighborhoods needed to be shoved aside, or obliterated. In lieu of sensitivity to "character of place," a completely alien, North American-style project was built here. The model was said to be Battery Park City in New York. But Battery Park, adjacent to Wall Street, fits compactly into and follows the traditional street pattern of Manhattan. Canary Wharf is six miles from the City and downtown London, in what is now an alien setting.

Canary Wharf, with a £5-billion price tag, bankrupted the world's largest development company, Olympia & York of Toronto, said to have sunk £2.2 billion into Europe's biggest development. There were reports in 1995 of increased office occupancy, suggesting that the worst on the financial side may be past, but in mid-1995 the signature tower, One Canada Square, tallest in Europe at seventy stories, was still only sixty percent occupied.[4]

Another example of flawed planning is the newly opened up old port area in Barcelona, with its otherwise elegant public waterfront spaces and cafes. Plans for the redevelopment of Port Vell, which include an aquarium, IMAX theater, "festival marketplace" and cruise-ship terminal, appear to mimic North American models with architecture that does not take full advantage of the splendid harborfront site.

Hong Kong's Tsin Sha Tsui Cultural Center on the Kowloon waterfront represents another major missed chance for a dramatic waterfront presence. The building presents enormous blank walls to one of the world's most spectacular harbors, though a plaza with a viewing platform at least gives the public access to the water's edge. Likewise, plans for a major redevelopment project in Macau appear to skimp greatly on public access to the waterfront.

Unsuccessful waterfront projects can also be observed in such American cities as Baltimore, where a shoreline urban amusement venue failed and high-rise condominiums are out of scale with the harborfront. Furthermore, many riverfront cities in the United States are currently being overrun with unsightly casinos and adjoining parking lots. The Biloxi, Mississippi, waterfront is adulterated with windowless boxes on pilings, which house gambling operations. Flint, Michigan, Minneapolis, New Orleans and Toledo, Ohio, are further examples of cities where waterfront festival marketplaces did not succeed, and their failures led to a loss of interest in such projects in the America in the late 1980s.

The central Boston waterfront is home to Rowe's Wharf, center left, a successful mixed-use development that is a new gateway to the downtown area (see pp. 60–5).

21

WHAT IS "ON" THE WATERFRONT?

It is interesting to consider what is meant by "on" the waterfront. Our view is that the answer about whether or not a project is on the waterfront is basically psychological—does it *feel* like it relates to the water or is intrinsically part of the city's waterfront as a whole?

Quincy Market in Boston is classed as a "waterfront" project. Yet, it is actually eight hundred feet from the present-day harbor, and the view to and from the water has been blocked for more than thirty years by an overhead expressway. In the early history of Boston, boats actually tied up here, but like many cities Boston filled its bays and marshes to create new land and development opportunities. A good case could be made that Quincy Market is not in fact "on" the waterfront of Boston Harbor. Faneuil Hall and Quincy Market are nonetheless central and lively components of Boston's overall downtown waterfront revival. When the expressway is put underground and covered by a park, the link of Quincy Market to the waterfront will be more obvious.

Pike Place Market in Seattle sits well above the waterfront there, separated from it by an elevated expressway and railroad line, but affords excellent views of the sound. The cafes and restaurants of Marseille are also divided from the water by a roadway and extensive marinas, yet they seem much a part of the waterfront scene.

Consider the Exhibition Centre, the Chinese Garden and the museums of Darling Harbour, Sydney (see pp. 40–3). Physically they are remote from Cockle Bay and functionally have little to do with the water, although water elements have been creatively introduced in ponds and fountains throughout the project. Yet these facilities are a prominent part of a massive waterfront redevelopment undertaking, the audacious makeover of Darling Harbour, once a near-downtown rail yard served by ships. Are these projects "on" the waterfront? Yes and no.

Our selections in *The New Waterfront* are all "on" the waterfront in the sense that they themselves, or the project they are part of, embrace the water body in question. Well-executed waterfront redevelopments should reflect and celebrate the character of their location and city. Today, we have a pervasive international architectural style (variously modern and postmodern) that threatens to obliterate local character. We have chain stores springing up everywhere with products and appearances so similar that it is difficult to tell whether you are in Singapore, Chicago or London.

On the other hand, there are projects that do fit congenially into their locale and enhance their cities, and it is these we celebrate here. For instance, at the Forks Renewal in Winnipeg, Manitoba, Canada, located at the confluence of the Assiniboine and the Red Rivers where the city was founded, a complex of carefully restored railroad buildings and a variety of entertainment venues immediately give the visitor a sense of the character of this northern plains city (see pp. 116–7).

At particular sites, projects that "fit" can also be bold architectural statements. Along the Moll de la Fusta in Barcelona, a wonderfully wide promenade has been constructed that skillfully obscures parking and roadways and features benches and walls in splendid tile designs. It is all handsomely landscaped

22

The Louisville Falls Fountain illuminates the Ohio River and the Humana Building, left.

and there is a restaurant decorated with whimsical crayfish sculpture. In the whole development you sense the character of this special place, where good design and a lively public realm is a high civic virtue. In another successful scheme, at the striking Harumi Passenger Terminal in Tokyo Harbor, a new public attraction has been created, affording dramatic harbor and city views, and a once-isolated waterfront precinct has been adopted into the fabric of the city (see pp. 172–5).

The projects chosen illustrate one of our most strongly felt views, namely, that each community is and must remain for its own sake, unique and distinctive in its character, history, economy and political leadership. When well-designed and executed, the waterfront venues around the globe respond to this instinct and create schemes that grow from and reflect the spirit and aspirations of the city they are meant to enhance. The successes of the new urban waterfront signal, then, a basic desire not only to get to or near the water but to live, work and play in, and to be part of healthy, stimulating cities.

A restaurant on one of two islands that house authentic Chinese and Japanese gardens on Jurong Lake in Singapore and pose a serene contrast to neighboring apartment towers.

CHAPTER *1*

Major Waterfront
Transformations

Rising from the debris of old piers, out of the rubble of discarded (or bombed) industrial factories, and emerging from fenced-off precincts or on newly created land, major waterfront transformations are occurring around the globe today. They include some of the most dramatic redevelopment projects of our time, and they reflect the startling ability of cities to adapt to altered economic and social circumstances.

Typically involving hundreds of acres—a few consist of thousands—these projects are generally tied to, and sometimes lead the way in, city-center rejuvenation. Complex negotiations, dedicated leadership and huge sums of public and private money are involved. The projects are highly visible and usually touch some chord in the city's industrial or cultural heritage.

Of all the major waterfront transformation stories, Baltimore's Inner Harbor has become the classic tale of modern times. Numerous cities in various countries have the stated aim of becoming "like Baltimore." These include such prominent cities as Sydney and Barcelona. The Darling Harbour project in Sydney was consciously modeled on the Inner Harbor. Barcelona officials acknowledge that their current Old Port project is modeled on Baltimore. And the cycle continues, with the Puerto Madero project in Buenos Aires, in turn, looking to Barcelona for inspiration.

What, then, is Baltimore's waterfront transformation about? It is a unique story of business and political leadership coming together at a particular juncture in the history of a distinctive American city that enjoys a close association with its main water body, the upper reaches of the Chesapeake Bay. The Inner Harbor's successful combination of features, serving both a resident downtown business community and a major tourist population, makes it difficult to imagine today the hapless conditions that existed in the 1960s.

The scheme currently includes, among other things, a nearby convention center, a major hotel, office towers, festival marketplaces, paddleboats, a science museum, a large park, restaurants, a major aquarium, a small hotel, ferries, tour boats, condominiums, public art installations, a nearby baseball stadium and newly opened biotechnology research center, all keyed to a thirty-five-foot-wide, brick promenade, open at the water's edge, that surrounds the small harbor basin and is part of an expanding harbor walkway.

As exemplary and inspiring as the Baltimore story is, Baltimore is *not*, in our view, a "model" or "magic formula" any more than Granville Island in Vancouver, Canada, the Victoria & Alfred Waterfront in Cape Town, South Africa, or Teleport City in Tokyo are "models." Rather, these transformations are unique expressions that meet the needs and aspirations of cities that are unlike in geography, history and character. They share many common factors—housing, shopping, recreation, office and education, space, etc.—and each of these projects produced both positive and negative results that other cities can learn from. For one city to copy blindly the particular approach of another, however, is to risk disaster.

"Major transformation" does not always mean big; such schemes can be relatively small in size, as in the case of the Providence, Rhode Island, USA, and Birmingham, UK, projects, but we include them among major projects because of their impact and symbolic value.

Whatever the motivating force—be it the visionary mayor, passionate citizens' group, determined business community, persistent architect or far-seeing government agency—the waterfront transformations depicted here are generally bold and dramatic. Many have had a significant effect on the civic psyche, touching as they do the souls of their cities and giving renewed pride to their residents.

OPPOSITE: **An aerial view of the Inner Harbor of Baltimore, with the aquarium (on the pier), the World Trade Center, right, and the twin Harborplace marketplace structures, center.**

> *Let the river roll which way it will, cities will rise on its banks.*
> Ralph Waldo Emerson, *Journals*

See these projects in the Gazetteer:

Baltimore Inner Harbor, USA
Duluth Waterfront, USA
Battery Park City, New York, USA
Granville Island, Vancouver, Canada
Takeshiba Pier, Tokyo, Japan
Cardiff Inner Harbour, Wales
Dublin Custom House Docks, Ireland
Genova Aquarium, Italy
Granary Wharf, Leeds, UK

SOME MAJOR WATERFRONT TRANSFORMATIONS

Project/City	Size	Cost	Former Use	Date
Granville Island Vancouver	42 acres	$70 million	industry	1979
Harbourfront Toronto	90 acres	$340 million	industry/rail	1972
Battery Park City New York	92 acres	$4 billion	land fill	1979-
Inner Harbor Baltimore	95 acres	$2.5 billion	port	1963-
Port Vell Barcelona	134 acres	$340 million	port	u.c.
Salford Quays Manchester	148 acres	$750 million	port	1990
Darling Harbour Sydney	148 acres	$2.5 billion	abandoned rail	1988
Victoria & Alfred Cape Town	203 acres	R.2.5 billion	docklands/ industry	1989
Kop von Zuid Rotterdam	308 acres	DFl.475 million (public money)	port/industry	u.c.
Minato Mirai 21 Yokohama	460 acres	$200 billion	landfill	1983-
OJ Havengebied Amsterdam		$2.5 billion	old docks	1989-
Teleport City Tokyo	1,107		landfill	u.c.
Docklands London	5,000 acres		warehouses/ docks	1981-

u.c. under construction

PACIFICO YOKOHAMA

Yokohama,
JAPAN

project name	Pacifico Yokohama
water body	Yokohama Bay
size	100,558 square meters
cost	$100 million
completion date	1991–94
sponsor	Pacifico Yokohama Corp. with Japanese Government and Yokohama City
designers	Nikken Sekkei, Tokyo
	Mancini-Duffy, Associates, New York
contact person	Mr. Goro Fukumori
	Pacifio Yokohama
	1-1-1 Minato Mirai
	Nishi-ku, Yokohama 220
	JAPAN
	Tel. 81 24 221 2124
	Fax 81 45 221 2136

The Pacifico Yokohama project—four integrated buildings plus a public park at a prime waterfront site —is a signature of the vast Minato Mirai 21 undertaking, a virtually new city in the center of one of Japan's largest metropolitan areas.

Minato Mirai 21 covers 460 acres and is considered to be among Japan's largest urban redevelopment undertakings. Every dimension is staggering. Already present is Japan's tallest building, Landmark Tower (seventy stories), a project of Mitsubishi Estate Co. Ltd., which contains a luxury hotel, an upscale shopping center and offices.

ABOVE: **The 31-story Yokohama Grand Inter-Continental Hotel dominates the Pacifico Yokohama project.**

BELOW: **The site plan of the ambitious 460-acre Minato Mirai 21 scheme.**

When completed by the target date of the year 2000, Minato Mirai 21 will house 10,000 residents and handle a work force of 190,000. Backed by the Japanese government, and overseen by the Yokohama Minato Mirai 21 Corporation, the entire project is a vast public-private partnership. The initial budget estimate was 2 trillion yen, approximately $200 billion.

At the leading edge of the entire project, in location and architectural design, is Pacifico Yokohama. The project's signature building is a gracefully curved, thirty-one-story hotel, the Yokohama Grand Inter-Continental. A five-star facility with six hundred rooms, its white sail-like shape points into the harbor, providing panoramic views of the waterfront, the surrounding city and nearby Mt. Fuji. Its geometric form is an effective contrast with the heavy-handed Landmark Tower nearby. Integrated with the hotel are three large meeting facilities. A conference center and the National Convention Hall of Yokohama wrap around the hotel. Adjoining is the separate but architecturally integrated Exhibition Hall.

The conference center, seven stories stepped down to the waterfront, has nearly sixty meeting rooms, including a hall that holds one thousand people and a smaller auditorium for 390. A wide public walkway along the harbor unites the conference center, hotel and adjacent convention hall.

The latter facility is a joint venture of Mancini Duffy Associates of New York together with Nikken Sekkei Ltd. of Tokyo, who designed the hotel, conference center and exhibition hall. The convention hall has an

ABOVE: **An overall view of the Pacifico Yokohama project, with the hotel, left, convention and exhibit halls, right.**

LEFT: **A historic vessel and Ferris wheel frame the Grand Inter-Continental Hotel.**

RIGHT: **A view of the hotel from the harbor shows the conference center on either side.**

FAR RIGHT: **The Landmark Tower, left, at 70 stories is Japan's tallest building. At center and right are the four components of Pacifico Yokohama.**

RIGHT: **Graceful curves dominate the conference center entrance.**

BELOW: **The glass-fronted Exhibition Hall faces the harbor against the Convention Hall in the background.**

auditorium that seats five thousand. Its remarkable features include a simultaneous translation system that is capable of handling as many as eight languages. Unusual for such facilities are its notable orientation to the harbor, large seaside lobby, extensive plaza and complete glass frontage.

The fourth building of the complex is the huge, white Exhibition Hall, which contains ten thousand square meters of column-free space. The delicate, sail-like wings across the roof add a playful note on the waterfront. In front of the Exhibition Hall is a large public space, Seaside Park, which has a terrace at the water's edge.

Basic plans for Minato Mirai 21 were announced in 1979 and detailed planning was finished two years later. Infrastructure development then began, which included a new rail station and Nippon-maru Park, with its historic vessel, which opened in 1985 (see p. 202). The conference center/hotel followed in August 1991, the exhibition center several months later and the auditorium in 1994. The Landmark Tower opened in 1993, joining numerous other facilities—both private offices and an art and maritime museum—now built and operating. One of the most impressive aspects of Minato Mirai 21 is that such a vast undertaking is proceeding precisely on schedule. When finished, the soaring white shape of the Pacifico hotel and its handsome surrounding buildings will no doubt remain the visual symbol of a totally remade city district.

RIGHT: **A night view of the National Convention Hall of Yokohama, which seats 5,000.**

BELOW: **A rear view of the Grand Inter-Continental Hotel shows the Conference Hall at its base.**

BOTTOM: **A generous public walkway leads to the front of the Convention Hall.**

ABOVE AND RIGHT: **The tiered levels of the Conference Hall form a dramatic contrast with the plain façade of the Grand Inter-Continental Hotel.**

RIVER RELOCATION PROJECT

Providence,
Rhode Island, *USA*

Waterplace is the heart of the dramatic $40-million river relocation project helping to transform downtown Providence.

project name	Downtown River Relocation
water body	Woonasquatucket, Moshassuck and Providence rivers
size	35 acres
cost	$40 million
completion date	1987–
sponsor	Rhode Island Dept. of Transportation/ City of Providence
designers	William D. Warner, Architects and Planners
contact person	William Warner
	William D. Warner, Architects and Planners
	595 Ten Rod Road
	Exeter, Rhode Island, 02882
	USA
	Tel. 1 401 295 8851 Fax 1 401 294 5581

"A Riverfront Transformed" read the headline of the January 10, 1993, edition of the *Providence Sunday Journal*. No exaggeration this, for what has taken place in the heart of the gritty old city of Providence, Rhode Island, is truly dramatic. It is one of the most audacious—and least known—downtown waterfront undertakings anywhere.

Born of a waterfront study launched in 1983, and tied to other major downtown projects, such as a new, relocated railroad terminal and a new convention center, the key concept was to remove the decking that covered the Providence River. In conjunction with this plan the courses of the Woonasquatucket and Moshassuck rivers, where they flow together to form the Providence River, were to be relocated, freeing space for a crucial downtown roadway. The waterfront plan also advanced a larger previous scheme, drawn up in 1980, which had designated a "Waterplace" park in the middle of a thirty-five-acre

renewal area but which had no funding in place and had not addressed the problem of the rivers.

The river relocation proposal, advanced by architect William Warner, would be a bold initiative for any city, but was especially so in a relatively small (population 170,000) and somewhat depressed city that was generally overlooked because of its location between the major magnets of New York and Boston. The city's key assets are its large university population (Brown University, Providence College, and the Rhode Island School of Design are located in Providence) and a strong arts community. These factors and the availability of Federal highway funds help explain the receptivity to what otherwise would surely have struck many as a wild idea.

However, after an expenditure of $40 million and six years of relocation work, the downtown rivers were, in fact, moved into new channels, eight feet deep and several hundred feet from their previous

locations. Where once a single deck, known as the world's widest bridge (in the *Guinness Book of Records*), covered a stretch of the Providence River there are now eight graceful new bridges; each has been individually designed and skillfully arched to accommodate boat traffic. The entire project includes twelve new bridges.

River relocation made possible an extension of Memorial Boulevard, which runs where the Woonasquatucket once flowed, to help ease traffic circulation downtown. Indeed, the project was originally known as the Memorial Drive Extension, for which highway funds were allocated. The rivers, located below grade as they are, have now become ideal locations for pedestrian walkways. Here architect Warner drew inspiration from the exquisite design details of the Paseo del Rio in San Antonio (see p. 193). The walkways are surfaced in a variety of pavings and demonstrate a careful selection of street

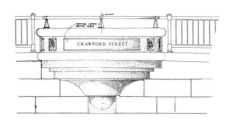

furniture (lamp posts, garbage receptacles, railings, etc.), clear directional signs and other attention to detail that signals a project thoughtfully and artfully planned.

The general treatment of the newly opened public spaces, centering on the four-acre Waterplace at the western end of the walkway network, combines brick, heavy granite and wrought iron, with new landscaping. As a final detail, educational plaques and graphic panels help tell the story of Providence's waterfront history. A visitor's center and restaurant as well as an amphitheater and smaller plazas are all part of this segment. Boats are now able to use the upper portion of the rivers, beginning at Waterplace. A ferry to Newport, Rhode Island, is also planned to operate from here.

Along the reopened rivers downtown, a number of commercial projects have been built. A bank headquarters is at the confluence point, where the relocated rivers form the Providence River, as is a small public park. Apartment buildings have gone up nearby, some retail and office activity has moved into the old railroad station area and the new convention center/hotel has been completed.

The make-over of downtown Providence continues. The proposed relocation of an interstate highway will free up more riverfront property. The city center is now a gem of public space that will in all likelihood age gracefully and attract new adherents as more development occurs in the area. This will no doubt contribute to one of the intangible achievements of the project—a boost in civic pride.

LEFT: **Former train station structures are gradually being converted to new uses.**

ABOVE: **A detail of the Crawford Street pedestrian bridge across the Providence River.**

BELOW AND BOTTOM: **Graceful, well-detailed bridges are a hallmark of the project.**

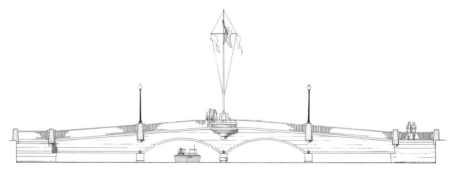

33

ABOVE: **A wide pedestrian underpass connects to the Old Union Station complex. Waterplace is in the distance.**

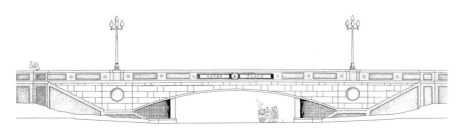

AKER BRYGGE

Oslo,
NORWAY

project name	Aker Brygge
water body	The Oslofjord
size	160 acres
cost	$350 million (Phase II)
completion date	1980–
sponsor	Aker Brygge ANS
designers	Telje - Torp - Aasen Arkitektkontor A/S; Tom Ottar A/S; Bergersen, Gromholt og Ottar Arketektkontor and Kleven Almaas Wike (Phase I) Niels Torp A/S (Phase II); Arkitektkontoret Kari Nissen Brodtkorb (Phase III)
contact person	Paul Moen Bryggedrift A/S Holmans Gate 4 0250 Oslo NORWAY Tel./Fax 47 22 8326 2680

Built in three distinct phases, by three different architectural practices, Aker Brygge is a vibrant mix of bold new architecture and rehabilitated shipyard buildings that constitutes virtually a new downtown for Oslo.

The wide promenade, which runs the full length of the project along the quay and is lined with cafes, restaurants and restaurant/cruise boats, is thronged in summer months. For winter use there are interior walkways, protected pockets and attractive indoor spaces, and a plaza within the project is animated with outdoor cafes in good weather. The promenade is the scene of street dancing in summer. The development collectively now attracts an estimated six million people annually.

Two conditions in the early 1980s set the stage for Aker Brygge, which is now one of Europe's premier waterfront conversions. The first was the closing down of the Nyland shipyard after 130 years of operation, with the loss of as many as two thousand jobs. The shipyard's owner, Aker a.s., initiated the redevelopment through a new company, Aker Brygge ANS. The second critical step was the relocatiion of a major roadway in a tunnel running beneath the site and the adjoining City Hall plaza. Historic photos show massive traffic congestion in the area prior to the construction of the tunnel, which effectively cut off City Hall from the Oslo Bay. When the problem of congestion was removed, the prospect of developing this

ABOVE: **An aerial view of the Aker Brygge complex at the head of Oslofjord, with downtown Oslo behind it.**

BELOW: **Popular cafes are located below the 120-unit apartment/commercial building.**

RIGHT: **A dramatic office/retail and apartment structure, one of 11 buildings in Aker Brygge, is among those surrounding Bryggetorget, the project's main plaza.**

prime area became more obvious. An open competition for proposed schemes was held in 1982, entitled "The City and the Fjord Oslo Year 2000" and it inaugurated the process of serious planning.

Another important feature that the tunneling made possible is a car-free zone. While not always a successful gambit, it works at Aker Brygge, in part because downtown is in immediate proximity and because there were strong efforts to make the pedestrian links numerous and prominent. Furthermore, an excellent public transit system serves downtown Oslo.

Phase I began at the City Hall end of the quay and was completed in 1986. There are three principal buildings, two restorations and a new structure housing retail and offices. Included are a theater and theatrical academy.

Phase II was double the scope, with 100,000 square meters of space in four major new buildings and a festival square. Whereas the first work is dominated by the handsome former shipyard buildings,

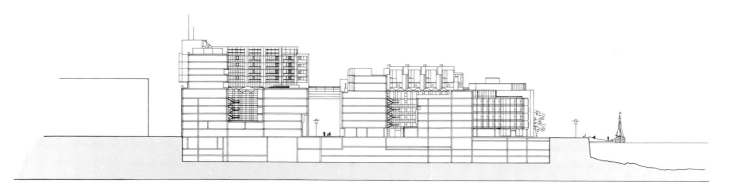

The cross-section shows underground parking for 1,600 vehicles, which extends under the dock .

SECTION
AKER BRYGGE II
MÅLESTOKK: 1:500
10m   0m   30m

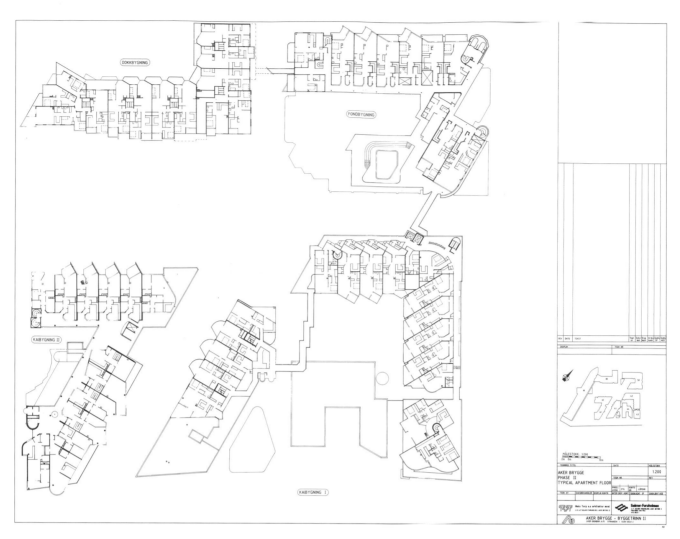

A site plan of Phases II and III at Aker Brygge shows the main plaza at top and a second alley to the harbor at bottom left.

Phase II consists of striking modern structures that are artfully arrayed, with passageways running between them and providing strong sight lines toward the bay. A substantial marina was part of the development as well. There are shops on the first levels, office space at the intermediate levels and apartments on top with spectacular views of the working harbor. There are two movie houses, a theater, a health center and a kindergarten. Office space is again the predominant use, but, as in the first phase, the street level is devoted to public attractions.

The final stage of the project, Phase III, is a well-designed apartment structure containing 120 units and a small amount of office space. It, too, features shops and restaurants at ground level. Such was the popularity of the scheme that the majority of the units were sold during early construction. Stranden A/S was completed in 1990 and was voted the favorite new building in Oslo in a newspaper poll. A parking garage runs beneath the project and has 1,600 spaces, a large number for Oslo.

The whole development of Aker Brygge includes a cluster of eleven separate buildings that are bound together, despite multiple owners (there are 350 apartments in total) and uses, in a unique management district. A private company, Bryggedrift A/S, manages the complex and handles many traditional municipal functions.

The project is also visually unified. Its buildings are relatively small, and they work together in large part because of similarities in scale and/or color, or because they contrast pleasingly with each other. For the public, the streetscape is free-flowing and inviting; the spaces have a feeling of intimacy, and there are numerous passageways through and between buildings. A view of Oslo Bay is never far away, and along

LEFT: **A water sculpture is surrounded by bricked berms that serve as seating and play areas in pleasant weather.**

BELOW: **Fountains and public art pieces enliven the main pedestrian plaza.**

the quay a handsome forty-foot-wide walkway steps down to the water.

A great advantage of the project, something not common to all such developments, is that as many as five thousand people are employed at Aker Brygge now. They are not in the scarce blue-collar jobs to be sure, but they constitute twice the number employed when Aker was a shipyard.

ABOVE: **The harborside Stranden A/S complex features shops, offices, restaurants and apartments.**

BELOW LEFT: **The Dokkbygget apartment building faces onto a former shipyard.**

RIGHT: **A pedestrian bridge over a former dry dock connects Aker Brygge's plaza to Tjuvholmen Pier.**

LEFT: **A detail shows how the apartments are cantilevered over a walkway.**

TOP RIGHT: **Steps at water's edge are a popular gathering spot.**

BELOW: **A harborside view of the Stranden A/S complex and wide public walkway.**

DARLING HARBOUR

Sydney,
New South Wales, *AUSTRALIA*

project name	Darling Harbour/Sydney Exhibiton Centre
water body	Darling Harbour
size	148 acres
cost	$2.5 billion; $80 million (Exhibiton Centre)
completion date	1988
sponsor	Darling Harbour Authority
designer	Keys Young (master plan); Philip Cox, Richardson Taylor and Partners (Exhibition Centre)
contact person	Di Talty, Darling Harbour Authority Level 16 2 Market Street Sydney, NSW 2000 Australia Tel. 61 2 286 0100 Fax 61 2 286 0199

ABOVE: **Cockle Bay is at the heart of the 148-acre Darling Harbour project; the historic Pyrmont Bridge is at right.**

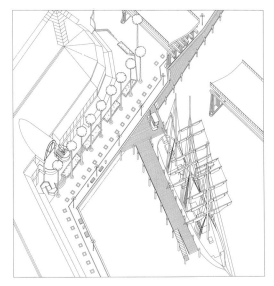

LEFT: **A detail of the impressive public walkway system that is a principal feature of Darling Harbour.**

For more than one hundred years, the principal rail-to-sea interchange in Sydney was based at Darling Harbour, at the edge of the downtown business district. In a now-familiar pattern, downtown congestion in conjunction with technological developments led to the government-owned rail yard being moved in 1982.

Building on planning studies that dated back as early as 1971, a decision was made by New South Wales Premier Neville Wran to redevelop the area as a public entertainment district, as the state's contribution to Australia's bicentennial observance in 1988. In less than four years, then, the industrial/transportation heritage of 196 years was completely transformed into a "people place" that is now one of Australia's most visited locations.

From the beginning the scheme was designed to include an exhibition center and convention building, a Chinese Garden (Sydney's Chinatown lies to the south), the National Maritime Museum, a hotel and a harborside market. Nearly everything on the site—a pumphouse that is now a pub is the exception—was demolished for the make-over.

An independent Darling Harbour Authority was put in place in autumn 1984 by the state and given major authority, reporting officially to the minister for public works while maintaining an unofficial liaison with the city government (the arrangement ran into criticism locally). Consultants were hired to serve as the design directorate (MSJ Keys Young) and as managing contractors (Leighton Contractors), and they were overseen by a quality review committee. The entire scheme was put on the fast track to meet a January 1988 deadline.

LEFT: **A wide, unfenced public promenade in front of the Harbourside market opens to Cockle Bay**

BELOW: **A sketch of the Pier Street Underpass shows the historic Pumphouse Tavern at right and *Stonehenge*, an art piece, foreground.**

41

The result, largely completed by the extraordinary deadline but significantly embellished since, is an urban entertainment zone whose outstanding characteristic is generous and carefully designed public spaces. A monorail and water ferry help tie the precinct into the downtown and to overcome the barrier of the highway.

Among the attractions are, most significantly, the bay itself. Around it are arrayed various installations, the principal being the Harbourside festival market. This is very much on the US model; James Rouse of Columbia, Maryland, the marketplace guru, was a consultant and the late Mort Hoppenfeld, the Rouse Co. director of design, took part. The Harbourside architect was RTKL of Baltimore, Maryland.

What distinguishes Harbourside is the amount and variety of restaurants and cafes that are open to Darling Harbour, with dramatic views toward the central business district as well as over the harbor where nearby shipping operations are visible. There is a maritime museum, an aquarium, three hotels, an office complex and a convention center oriented to the bay. All of these structures surround a wide, brick promenade that is completely open to the water.

Facing inland, under the freeway barrier that is nicely masked by the use of water features and

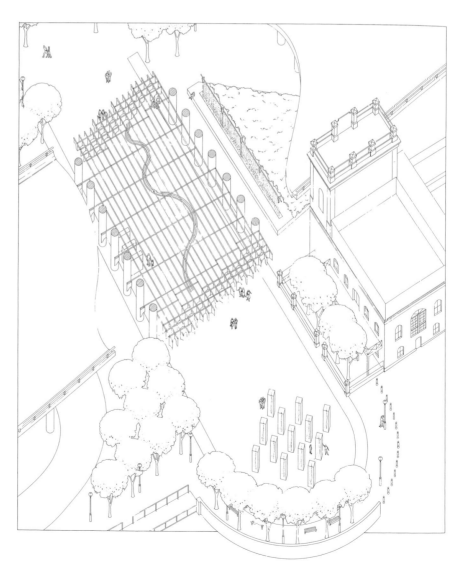

LEFT: **Competitors in the Dragon Boat race, one of many annual events at Darling Harbour, pass in front of the Australian National Maritime Museum.**

landscaping, there is a substantial green space, Tumbalong Park, a small lake, Chinese Garden (a quiet oasis), a major, 250,000-square-foot exhibition center of striking design (see p. 204) and the Pumphouse Tavern. Immediately adjacent and effectively part of the attractions at Darling Harbour is the Pumphouse Museum of Applied Arts and Sciences, which is housed in a converted powerhouse.

Public response has been widely positive. Even critics concede that the enterprise is a success, as visitor numbers nearing fifteen million (seventy percent of whom are locals) suggest. The British publication *Architectural Review* styled the project as suburban, escapist, even anti-urban. For the reviewer, the absence of a street grid, housing and serious places of work was critical. (In fact, a huge industrial structure

overlooking Darling Harbour is currently being converted to apartments and an office complex is already in place, housing IBM, among other companies.)

This criticism overlooks the context. Darling Harbour is a public playground similar to the Tivoli Garden in Copenhagen. The lively downtown area, the neighborhood of Pyrmont, which is now being redeveloped, the historic district of The Rocks (see pp. 132–5) and the spectacular Opera House (see pp. 112–3) and Botanic Gardens are all close by. It is this array of different public attractions opening to Sydney Harbour and surrounding the core central business district, all of which are readily accessible, that make this project a fine fit for one of the world's great waterfront cities.

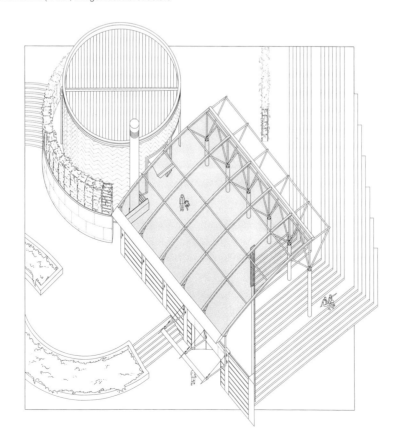

ABOVE: **Pyrmont Bridge spans Darling Harbour. The maritime museum is at lower right, Harbourside and the convention center are at right, facing the harbor, and the aquarium and ferry dock are at lower left.**

LEFT: **A sketch of the Palm Pavilion shows its transparent roof.**

ASIA AND PACIFIC TRADE CENTER

Cosmo Square,
Osaka, *JAPAN*

project name	Asia and Pacific Trade Center
water body	Osaka Bay
size	18 acres; 395 acres (Cosmo Square)
cost	$4.3 billion (Cosmo Square)
completion date	1994
sponsor	ATC Corporation
designers	Nikken Sekkei Ltd.,Tokyo; EDAW, Inc.,
	San Francisco (landscape)
contact person	Isao Osumi
	Port and Harbor Bureau
	2-8-24 Chikko Minato-ku
	Osaka 552 JAPAN
	Tel. 81 6 572 5121 Fax 81 6 572 0554

The 450-meter long, stepped and landscaped public promenade overlooks the bay and the Port of Osaka facilities.

Housed in a structure variously twelve and six stories in height, the Asia and Pacific Trade Center is a huge complex dedicated to wholesale trade. It occupies eighteen acres set amid a working port fronting Osaka Bay, and is a component of a sprawling new business district called Cosmo Square. What is remarkable for such a facility, where admission is generally restricted, is the major amount of public space provided; the handsomely landscaped prome-

44

RIGHT: **An aerial view shows the promenade leading to the 12-story Trade Mart, which houses the Design Center.**

nade along the bay is particularly noteworthy. The Trade Mart features a section of entertainment facilities, shops and restaurants that are open to the general public. Visitors may also enter the multiple levels of the International Trade Mart itself, but are not allowed to make purchases.

The structure, completed in 1994, cost $880 million and contains a total of 350,000 square meters of space. It features two atriums: one on the waterfront that is ten stories tall, the other breaking up the linear mass of the remaining structure and clearly marking a public entryway.

From the promenade, where generous seating at multiple levels is provided, there are spectacular and somewhat unusual views. Part of the container port of Osaka is nearby and in clear sight. There is an upper terrace promenade along the entire building that allows people to drop down a level or two to various

gardens, pavilions and fingerlike projections into the bay. There is a twenty-five-foot grade change overall from the building to the seawall. A "moon tower" is located at one end of the promenade where there are educational displays as well as an observation perch. A ferry dock here connects with the Osaka Aquarium and Suntory Museum (see pp. 94–7).

Within the complex, there are three principal zones. One is the Trade Mart itself, a second contains business support services (a trade promotion center, customs office and communications equipment), and the third houses what is called the "amenity zone," a cluster of restaurants and retail stores for the public and an indoor amusement center.

In one of its four sections, the Trade Mart contains the Design Center, which specializes in household appliances and furnishings. A second segment

ABOVE: **The promenade is open to the public.**

LEFT: **The central atrium of the Design Center, one of five atria in the complex, is 52 meters high and set off with vividly colored walls and girders.**

BELOW LEFT: **The Interior of Galaxy Square, part of a shopping/amusement/restaurant component that is open to the public.**

46

features sports, leisure and gift items, a third area is devoted to fashion and another to gems and jewelry.

The visual details are well executed. A bright red accent is used throughout the Asia and Pacific Trade Center and large amounts of glass break up the building mass. The building has a stepped white façade, and the whole effect is softened by an extensive planting of trees along the large bayfront promenade.

In the immediate vicinity of the Trade Center is a virtually new business zone of Osaka, where the fifty-five-story World Trade Center, or Cosmotower, dominates. Office towers for Itochu Corp., Sumitomo Corp. and Sumitomo Life Insurance Co. are in various stages of completion. A twenty-eight-floor Hyatt Regency is located nearby and a number of new, smaller offices fill out the rest of the area.

As large a developing area as it is (with over two hundred acres and additional reclaimed land due in 1996), Cosmo Square is only a portion of the truly staggering plans involving three huge areas of the port that amount to a total land area of 1,900 acres. Known as Technoport Osaka and due for completion in 2005, the waterfront is projected to have a residential population of 60,000, a work force of 92,000 and a daytime population of 200,000. The nearby Port Town development has already housed 32,000 people.

Cosmo Square, with the Asia and Pacific Trade Center at its bayfront, is the leading component of the ambitious Technoport project. Another segment will be Sports Island, containing, as the name suggests, an array of indoor and outdoor facilities for a population keenly interested in recreation and good health.

47

TOP: **Towering over the Asia and Pacific Trade Center is the 55-story Cosmo Tower, now complete. The training sail ship *Akogare* is moored here.**

ABOVE: **Dramatic steps lead down from Cosmo Gate Atrium to the water's edge.**

ABOVE LEFT: **On the north side of the Trade Mart is a mural, *Four Seasons*, by Yasukazu Tabuchi.**

LEFT: **Looking north along the popular promenade toward the Trade Mart.**

QUAYSIDE

Newcastle upon Tyne,
UK

project name	Quayside Development
water body	River Tyne
size	25 acres ("Newcastle Quayside")
cost	£160 million
completion date	1990–
sponsor	Tyne and Wear Development Corp.
	AMEC Developments
designers	Terry Farrell (master plan)
	Ove Arup and Partners (engineers)
contact person	Keith Bolton
	AMEC Developments
	Quayside
	Newcastle upon Tyne NE1 2PA
	UK
	Tel. 44 191 222 1010 Fax 44 191 261 6061

48

ABOVE: **Baltic Chambers, center, is a striking addition to the restored structures, left, part of the rebuilding of historic Quayside.**

LEFT: **The restored warehouse anchors the Newcastle Quayside redevelopment scheme. The riverfront here was previously lined with storage sheds.**

The Quayside, along the River Tyne, is situated down a sharp slope from the central business district, and has had a long and checkered history inextricably linked with the fortunes of Newcastle. Since the Middle Ages the economy of the whole region has been dependent upon the production of coal.

A major makeover has been successfully launched on the waterfront here, marking the beginning of a new chapter for the area. The new invest- ment of approximately £160 million coincides with a revival in the prosperity of Newcastle itself. The city is now the site of major new industrial investments, including a huge £1.1-billion pharmaceutical plant to be built by the Siemens corporation of Germany. The MetroCenter now has 350 stores and sees twenty- two million visitors a year.

The Quayside underwent a similarly thorough revamping during the Victorian era when a period of

LEFT: **Pandon Quays is a restored apartment complex with a corner pub located beside a new court structure.**

BELOW: **The new Copthorne Hotel and Bridge Court offices comprise a £30-million investment.**

major rebuilding followed the fire of 1854. As a result, the west end of Quayside contained prosperous offices, while warehouses dominated the east. In the usual pattern, however, the dockside lost its role over time as ships moved downstream and highways bypassed the docks. The industry that once thrived here also began to decline.

Since about 1990, the revival has been dramatic. On the west side is the well-designed Copthorne Hotel, which opened in 1991 with 156 rooms. An arcade fronts a wide landscaped walkway along the river. Next to the hotel is the Bridge Court office complex, which comprises two facing L-shaped buildings of multicolored brick and covers about seventy thousand square feet. Both the hotel and office complex were developed on derelict land that was enclosed by crumbling river walls.

The sloping hillside is the scene of another striking transformation in the area. Once a rubbish-strewn no-man's-land, it is now called the "Hanging Garden" and has walkways descending through it. Major plantings, stabilization walls and shrubs have also been added.

Refurbishment is proceeding along the central section of Quayside, where not many years ago deteriorated wharf structures lined the riverfront. A walkway is taking shape here now and the infill developments have begun to occupy the street frontage. The mixture of older buildings in the central waterfront on either side of the Tyne Bridge adds an interesting

ABOVE: **A new waterfront home for the Ouseborn Watersports Association.**

RIGHT: **The redeveloping Newcastle waterfront, with the classic River Tyne Bridge in the background, is the setting for a street fair.**

BELOW: **A sketch reveals the ambitious plan of the Newcastle Quayside development.**

diversity. The oldest building, now a large pub, has a small patio with river views. A handsome former fish market houses offices.

The most ambitious undertaking, the "Newcastle Quayside" project, lies to the east where development was launched in 1995 on a twenty-five-acre site stretching along the riverfront. Anchored by a major new courthouse and the redevelopment of Pandon Quays—warehouses refitted as apartments—the first of five new neighborhood squares was nearly completed at the end of 1995. Keelman Square, the first

to be built, features four office buildings, a pub/restaurant and a restored warehouse.

The master plan for Newcastle Quayside calls for an eventual 329,000 square feet of office space, 18,000 square feet of retail (such as pubs on the squares), 215 residences, a hotel and car parks. Envisioned is a Quayside cable-guided bus system, a walkway with landscaping and a major program of public art. The overall project cost is placed at about £170 million.

ABOVE LEFT: **Sandgate House, a new three-story office building, overlooks the River Tyne.**

LEFT: **Bridge Court office complex, next to the Copthorne Hotel, faces the public promenade along the river.**

BIRMINGHAM WATERFRONT

Birmingham,
UK

project name	Birmingham Waterfront
water body	Birmingham Canal
size	17 acres (Brindleyplace)
cost	£250 million (Brindleyplace)
completion date	1984–
sponsor	British Waterways, Birmingham City Council, Brindley Place, PLC
designers	Hatton Associates (Brindleyplace)
contact person	Tom Brock
	British Waterways
	Peel's Wharf, Lichfield Street
	Fazeley, Tamworth, Staffordshire B78 3QZ
	UK
	Tel. 44 1827 252 000
	Fax 44 1827 288 071

A vintage photograph reveals the forlorn state of Birmingham's canals before concerted public/private reinvestment occurred.

The transformation well under way in the center of Birmingham, England, could scarcely be more dramatic. Like many city centers, downtown Birmingham has suffered over the years from a variety of economic and social difficulties. Extensive bombing in World War II was followed by urban renewal, downtown ring roads, dreary architecture, unemployment and social problems. In addition there was the abandonment of a once-thriving canal network, deterioration in its water quality and the growing dereliction of nearby property.

What makes this development effort particularly outstanding is the fact that the vitality now so prevalent in the areas along the canals was such a bold reach at the time the plan was conceived. When announced initially by the Birmingham City Council, British Waterways and the private development known as Brindleyplace, there was no doubt strong skepticism that a project of this scope could work in Birmingham.

The improvement in water quality, added to the refurbishment of the canal towpath, locks and walls, where the Worcester and Birmingham Canal joins the Birmingham and Fazeley and Main Line Canals, is impressive in its own right. Today there are fish in the canals, thanks to a £2.2-million, three-year cleanup effort. After the removal of two hundred years' worth of accumulated pollutants, the National Rivers Authority has upgraded the canals from a 3 classification to 1b, one category below top water quality. A new convention center and indoor arena signal further investment.

Also well-launched is the companion private £250-million mixed-use project called Brindleyplace.

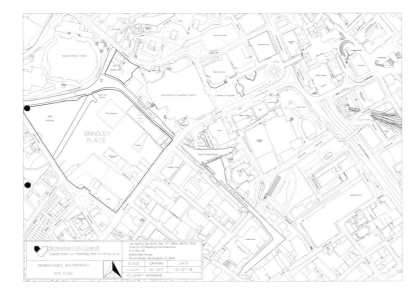

LEFT: **A map shows the canal system converging in central Birmingham.**

BELOW: **Gas Street Basin fell into disuse in the 1960s.**

ABOVE: **Birmingham's new International Convention Centre features a public plaza and walkways across from the Water's Edge commercial area.**

RIGHT: **A picturesque view through the gate of a restored canal building.**

BELOW: **The James Brindley pub and restaurant and colorful narrow boats enliven the new Gas Street Basin.**

A group of sixteen shops, restaurant/pubs and outdoor cafes called the Water's Edge is already thriving. Nearby are office buildings and new residential construction; a public aquarium, also under construction, is located immediately beside a major canal juncture. The full development calls for 1.1 million square feet of office space, 143 homes, a major public square, a 300-room hotel and 2,600 parking spaces, covering 17 acres in total.

The regeneration is already spreading into nearby areas; the Brindleyplace totals represent only part of the larger scheme that is coming into being. Regency Wharf, for example, a £5-million, thirty thousand-square-foot "leisure complex," involving extensive renovation of old canal structures, is under way nearby. Among other restoration work is the Malt House pub and the towpath bridges, which include a handsome iron structure dating from 1827.

There is also a Holliday Wharf Antiques Center, located in an old warehouse, and a boat-repair facility situated in a slightly funky area that contrasts with the bright new construction. Colorful tour boats carry visitors around the canals; joggers and walkers enjoy the finely detailed walkways which, incidentally, are unencumbered by railings.

Birmingham is the center of England's extensive canal network, the crossroads, as it were. Ten years ago the central waterfront was abandoned, the silt contaminated with heavy metals. The dramatic change taking place today in the center of Birmingham is evidence of what determination and willingness to invest in a central waterfront area can mean to a city. Where there once was a symbol of Birmingham's decline there are now Canal Sundays, and residents and as many as one million visitors per year come to enjoy a rebirth of the heart of the city.

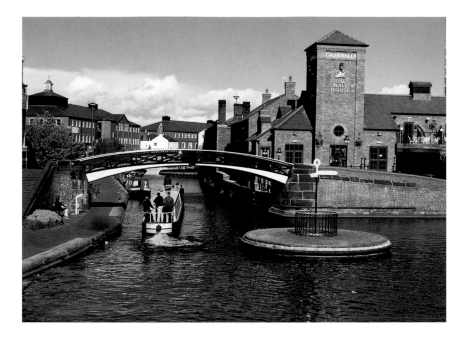

TOP: **One of several restored bridges, this connects the restaurants, shops and pubs of Water's Edge with the convention center.**

RIGHT: **A tour boat approaches The Malt House, a restored pub dating from 1780, at Canal Junction.**

FAR RIGHT: **Canal boats are moored downriver from the Hyatt Hotel.**

BELOW: **The Malt House, foreground, with the National Indoor Arena behind it.**

VICTORIA & ALFRED WATERFRONT

Cape Town,
SOUTH AFRICA

project name	Victoria & Alfred Waterfront
water body	Granger Bay
size	205 acres
cost	R. 2.5 billion
completion date	1988–
sponsor	Victoria and Alfred Waterfront (Pty) Ltd
designers	Gallagher Prinsloo and Associates
contact person	David Jack/P. S. Van Zyl
	Dock House, Dock House Road
	Victoria & Alfred Waterfront, P. O. Box 4416
	Cape Town 8000
	South Africa
	Tel. 27 21 418 2350
	Fax 27 21 25 4136

Victoria Wharf is the centerpiece restaurant and shopping complex that incorporates three old buildings on the Victoria & Alfred waterfront.

In a by-now familiar pattern the redevelopment of the Cape Town waterfront has attracted thirteen million visitors annually where once only a relative few ventured. The quality of planning and execution is, however, anything but ordinary.

The port authority took initiative in the late 1980s because it was losing money in a harbor area that had gradually been abandoned as changing technology relocated port functions and industry. The large Duncan Dock was often idle, and, as in the case of many cities, the waterfront had become increasingly cut off from the city center by highways and rail lines. At the same time, the historic central waterfront, the Pierhead Precinct, became an area of vitality, harboring recreational boats and the fishing fleet. These activities, including boat repair and more public amenities, maintained a core constituency and interest that helped call more general attention to the area's potential.

Agitation began in the early 1980s for redevelopment. According to David Jack, Victoria & Alfred Waterfront managing director and former Cape Town city planner, a catalyst was a Waterfront Steering Committee that was established by the mayor in 1984. In addition, a sixteen-day waterfront festival held at Pierhead that year enabled people, including government ministers, to visualize what might be accomplished.

The result was the setting up in late 1988 of the Victoria & Alfred Waterfront (Pty) Limited, a subsidiary of the state-owned transport corporation. Operations began in March 1989, with the land placed under long-term lease to the new corporation.

A plan was put forward in autumn 1989 that divided the more than two hundred acres into fourteen precincts and scheduled development to focus initially at Pierhead, in the very core of the harbor, and then to extend outward from the center in an orderly, organic way. The city developed a general framework and Victoria & Alfred was responsible for the rest, while a system was set up for approving individual precinct plans. Extensive public consultation was initiated and a public Liaison Committee established.

Work was allowed to get under way immediately at Pierhead, the commercial, cultural and historic center of the undertaking. To the existing scene of boating activity, which included an active tug harbor, were added a combination of restored and new facilities: restaurants and taverns (an old warehouse and equipment store became Ferryman's Tavern and Mitchell's Brewery), specialty shopping, a small hotel (sixty-eight rooms in a former warehouse), a theater, an arts-and-crafts market and the South African Maritime Museum as well as more boat slips. The 1904 Old Port Captain's Building became the waterfront company's offices and a restaurant. Infrastructure improvements were undertaken and a unified landscape design was introduced.

By the end of 1992, the Victoria Wharf retail and entertainment center (26,500 square meters) was opened and it proved to be a major public magnet. Phase III of the Pierhead redevelopment included an extension to Victoria Wharf, a three hundred-room hotel, an aquarium and an additional small-craft harbor. There are also a great many projects under way outside the core Pierhead area, including a Graduate

BELOW: **The Pierhead precinct features the Victorian architecture of the Old Port Captain's Building and the original Harbour Cafe.**

57

The Pierhead project area viewed from Victoria Wharf, with Table Mountain in the background.

School of Business, already in place, and a business park. Substantial housing is planned, as are major new retail spaces, including car sales centers and an IMAX theater.

Inevitably, much of the later work has been new construction. At the center of the Victoria & Alfred Waterfront, however, is a cluster of historic structures. Some of these are quite mundane old sheds, but they are now lively with new uses. The reused former harbor structures, along with an active working harbor, gives the Victoria & Alfred Waterfront project a certain authenticity and connection with the past that many other waterfront redevelopments have not had the opportunity—or perhaps the foresight—to include.

An active harbor is an appropriate setting for the restored 1902 Harbour Cafe.

CHAPTER 2

The Commercial
Waterfront

The commercial installations featured in this chapter have in common the capacity to encourage public enjoyment of the waterfront, for work, shopping or recreation. There are the obvious venues that feature an unbeatable combination of food, drink and a water view. Along with the classic waterfront seafood restaurant or venerable waterside tavern, we consider several more current expressions of this theme both in individual schemes—like a particularly high-style cafe/restaurant in Antwerp—and in components of larger complexes—in Toronto, Melbourne and Miami. Hotels that function as part of a larger mixed-use development, such as those in Portland, Oregon, and in Yokohama, Japan, likewise use their location to advantage.

There is but one example here of the "festival marketplace" in the mold popularized by the Rouse Co. of Maryland, USA. Architect/designers Benjamin and Jane Thompson collaborated with developer James Rouse first in Boston with Quincy Market, then with Harborplace in Baltimore, with South Street Seaport in New York and with Bayside in Miami, among other projects. The overly publicized formula they launched received exaggerated attention in the media and among academics. Regrettably this attention forged a permanent link in the public consciousness between the waterfront phenomenon in general and these particular festival marketplaces.

Rather than focus on one corporation's formula, which worked with spectacular and widely advertised success in relatively few places, we feature a variety of projects that naturally involve shopping and eating. There are derivative marketplaces that are variations on the Rouse theme, but more significant is the widespread and longstanding tradition of eating, shopping and socializing along water bodies, which predates the "festival marketplace" by centuries.

The Southgate commercial complex in Melbourne is a handsome dark-gray stone structure on the south bank of the Yarra River that fits in nicely with the distinctive architectural style of that city. With a wide, multilevel promenade and a number of cafes and restaurants fronting and overlooking the river, this popular spot helped give Melbourne a new identity and source of pride as well as a civic boost. By opening a new precinct for the city, the project typifies the dynamism of the commercial waterfront. Some would call this a "festival marketplace," but in doing so they would miss the distinctions between the popular formula and this iteration.

Queen's Quay Terminal on the waterfront in Toronto likewise is a public focal point, drawing people to eat and shop in its galleria, to attend cultural events in its dance theater, to work in its new offices and live in its top-floor condominiums. Some might also call this a "festival marketplace," but that term is not accurate here either. The Gabriel's Wharf area on the Thames in London (see Coin Street development, p. 212) is of a very different style and located in a festive, funky area where there are arts-and-crafts vendors and a number of other shops and cafes.

These and countless projects like them document the power of the well-planned, lively commercial waterfront. Such undertakings are not necessarily big or flashy; rather, many are contextual—architecturally, commercially and socially. Most importantly, the projects illustrated here demonstrate that the commercial tradition of waterfronts—where business in many forms has long been active—is continuing in a style that has been adapted to current needs.

The waterfront itself is the first wasted asset capable of drawing people at leisure. Part of the district's waterfront should become a great marine museum — the permanent anchorage of specimen and curiosity ship, the best collection to see and board anywhere. This would bring tourists into the district in the afternoon, tourists and people of the city on weekends and holidays, and in summertime it should be the embarkment point for pleasure voyages in the harbor and around the island; these embarkation points should be as glamorous and salty as art can make them. If new seafood restaurants and much else would not start up nearby, I will eat my lobster shell.

Jane Jacobs, *The Death and Life of Great American Cities,* 1961

OPPOSITE: **An architectural office/restaurant combination overlooks the Port of Hamburg.**

ROWE'S WHARF

Boston
Massachusetts, *USA*

project name	Rowe's Wharf
water body	Boston Harbor
size	5.4 acres
cost	$193 million
completion date	1987
sponsor	Rowe's Wharf Associates
designers	Skidmore Owings and Merrill
contact person	Bernard Dreiblatt
	Rowe's Wharf Associates
	Atlantic Avenue
	Boston, MA 02110
	USA
	Tel. 1 617 330 1400

The site plan of Rowe's Wharf, with the hotel,

right, shows the signature domed archway facing

Atlantic Avenue.

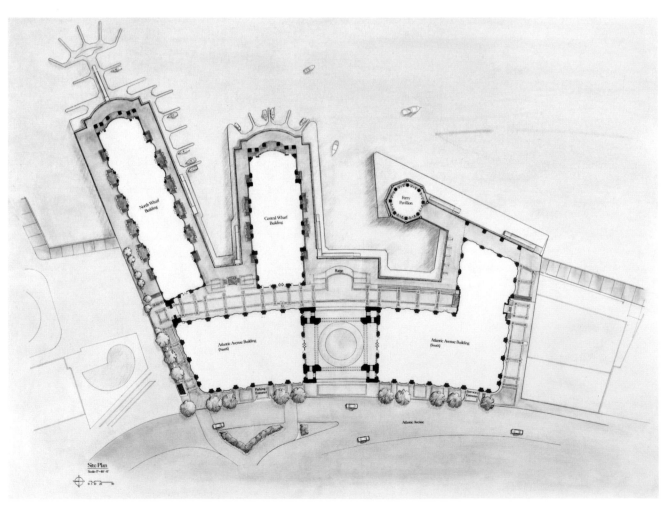

Site Plan
Scale 1" = 40'-0"

Rowe's Wharf on Boston Harbor, with ferry/excursion boat landings, left and center, condominiums on the pier at right and the Boston financial district in the background.

Rowe's Wharf, a mixed-use project on the central Boston waterfront, was completed in 1987 as the result of a collaboration between the city, developer, architect and design committee. The development was made possible by the fact that the city, in the name of the Boston Redevelopment Authority, owned the 5½-acre site. With Boston in the mid-1980s considered one of America's "hot" property markets, all participants wanted to make this a winning effort.

The fruit of the two-year collaboration is a carefully tiered design that embraces the waterfront setting. Rowe's Wharf consists of five separate components, including a luxury, 230-room hotel, 330,000 square feet of office space, 100 condominiums, a small retail

area, underground parking and an active dock, all woven together by a handsome brick exterior that corresponds well with the buildings in nearby downtown Boston.

The land side, on Atlantic Avenue, features two fifteen-story towers. In between these is the project's centerpiece, a 3½-story archway topped by a copper dome. Because of the view through the arch to and from the harbor, the project acts as a new gateway to the city. It makes a particularly dramatic welcome for travelers using the ferry service from the airport to Rowe's Wharf.

The project steps down toward the water in increments. Inside the twin towers the height is nine

OPPOSITE: **The interior of the Rowe's Wharf dome features a skylight and classical detailing.**

LEFT: **A construction detail of the archway with the waterfront façade at right, upper-level interior spaces, left, and copper dome.**

ABOVE AND BELOW: **A view from Atlantic Avenue through the 3½-story archway toward the harbor. A dockside boat kiosk is visible in the background.**

stories, conforming to older buildings in the area. The height of the structures then drops as you approach the water, to seven stories, and finally, at the water's edge, to three levels. All of these spaces enjoy spectacular harbor views.

As a project that features upper-income residential units and a luxury hotel, Rowe's Wharf could be an off-putting enclave. Several aspects guard against this kind of atmosphere. One of these features is the active dock, where commuter ferry services, including the airport service, and cruise ships are based. A second is the open archway and plaza area below, which give a welcoming sense of accessibility. A small, enclosed Belvedere-type structure punctuates one end of the dock, allowing people to escape bad weather while waiting for a ferry or just to enjoy harbor views in the winter.

Perhaps the most important element at Rowe's Wharf is the pleasant brick public walkway that surrounds the development. Action by the city in 1988 opened up an adjoining property to pedestrians, making way for a continuous waterfront connection in this area.

Not surprisingly, Rowe's Wharf has won high praise for its contextualist approach to fitting 665,000 square feet of space into the most historic section of downtown Boston.

ABOVE: **The Custom House clock tower, built in 1913, rises up behind Rowe's Wharf dome.**

FAR RIGHT: **The vernacular design of Rowe's Wharf blends well with the financial district and contrasts with the high-rise apartment towers, right, designed by I. M. Pei in 1971.**

RIGHT: **Looking down on the domed kiosk structure that functions as a shelter and waiting room for ferry and excursion boat passengers.**

BELOW: **The waterside kiosk, right, hotel, left, and clock tower at rear.**

RIVERPLACE

Portland,
Oregon, *USA*

project name	RiverPlace
water body	Willamette River
size	14.7 acres
cost	$209.5 million
completion date	1987
sponsor	Cornerstone Columbia Development Co., Seattle, and City of Portland
designers	Alan Grainger, GGLO, Seattle
	Olson Sundberg Architects, Seattle
contact person	Erma Dore
	GGLO Architecture and Interior Design
	1008 Western Avenue
	Seattle, WA 98104
	USA
	Tel./Fax 1 206 467 5828

RIGHT: **The site plan of RiverPlace, which fronts a new marina basin, with floating restaurant at lower left.**

BELOW: **RiverPlace, including the hotel at right, maintains a low profile against the downtown Portland skyline.**

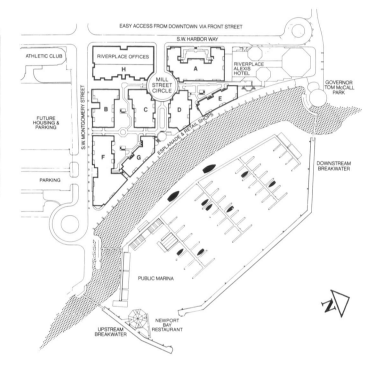

This mixed-use project sits on a ten-acre parcel of land that was carved out of a mile-long park beside the Willamette River in downtown Portland, Oregon. The Tom McCall Waterfront Park resulted from the most unusual action—for an American city, certainly—of removing a major highway. Harbor Drive Expressway had been the city's busiest roadway; the traffic now runs along the developing south bank of the river.

Expressway removal in 1976 enabled the downtown of Portland to be rejoined to the Willamette, which runs alongside it and flows into the Columbia River to the north. Anchoring one end of the mile-long greensward is a mixture of shops, restaurants, public promenade and town houses, offices, apartments, hotel and marina that was developed in two phases. RiverPlace cost a total of $200 million to build.

An initial public investment of $6 million provided for shore stabilization, the building of two breakwaters and a marina, and the construction of tree-lined roadways and connections to downtown. In 1983 a competition was held by the Portland Downtown Development Commission to find a single developer for the scheme. Cornerstone Columbia Development Co. of Seattle, Washington, won the commission and was presented with a plan and design guidelines.

The most successful aspect of the development is the combination of a fairly intense public space—a twenty-five-foot-wide, curved riverfront promenade above the marina, which is lined with small shops and restaurants—and private facilities, namely townhouse residences. Separation between the business and residential portions is achieved by a difference in

LEFT: **An interior courtyard of a residential component of RiverPlace is secluded from the public promenade.**

BELOW: **The marina office and floating restaurant at dock's end, with Marquam Bridge across the Willamette River in the background.**

elevation. In addition there are walls and gates, yet they avoid a fortress-like atmosphere. As a matter of public policy, which guards against public money being used to underwrite strictly high-end homes, an effort was made via land subsidy regulations to provide a number of middle-income housing units.

The two signature buildings of RiverPlace are the structures at either end: a small, luxury hotel, reminiscent in design of traditional seaside resort hotels and, on the opposite side, a health club facility that features a prominent clock tower. A floating restaurant, a marina, colorful dragon boats and tour vessels are all accessible by ramps and walkways and add a flurry of activity in the water area at the front of the project.

Cafes line the river side of the promenade, but ample room is left for pedestrians.

Much of the residential construction from the first phase is in wood, typical of building in the Pacific Northwest, while the office component is brick. Height is strictly controlled, with four-story structures predominating, so that the profile of the entire project fits well against the buildings rising in the downtown area immediately adjacent. Following the initial phase was the construction of apartment buildings on a nearby site.

The success of RiverPlace has led Portland to push ahead with plans for other residential, commercial and cultural developments on the river.

SOUTHGATE

Melbourne,
Victoria, *AUSTRALIA*

project name	Southgate
water body	Yarra River
size	6 acres
cost	Aus. $600 million
completion date	1994
sponsor	Jennings Industries
designers	The Buchan Group
contact person	David Cole
	The Buchan Group, Architects and Planners
	133 Rosslyn Street
	West Melbourne, Victoria 3003
	Australia
	Tel. 61 3 9329 1077
	Fax 61 3 9329 0481

OPPOSITE ABOVE: **A multilevel promenade provides a grand public space in front of the Southgate shopping/restaurant complex.**

OPPOSITE BELOW: **Looking west from Princes Bridge, Southgate presents a pleasing waterfront view.**

69

TOP: **The wide promenade along the Yarra River is a popular Southgate gathering place.**

LEFT: **The more austere face of downtown Melbourne is visible across the Yarra River.**

ABOVE: **A bold arch spans the new pedestrian bridge that connects downtown with Southgate.**

BELOW: **A classic riverside view of of the Melbourne skyline.**

The completion of the mixed-use Southgate project in 1992 on the south bank of the Yarra River in the middle of Melbourne has had a far greater impact than its six-acre size would suggest.

For years, the downtown portion of the Yarra was something to be avoided. Neglected and inaccessible as buildings and rail yards were built along it, and left to become a receptacle for waste and rubbish, the area was one of the city's greatest embarrassments.[1] Beyond its physical condition and muddy color, the Yarra had effectively divided Melbourne for years. On the south were industry, bogs and outlying suburbs, while immediately to the north was the classic Victorian Melbourne, the central business district.

Following a water cleanup, Southgate has succeeded in drawing people in large numbers across the river, uniting the two sides and kindling the spark of major new developments up and down the river. The Yarra has thus gone from being something of a divide to becoming a unifying feature. Because Southgate adjoins the Victorian Arts Centre there is now a combination of cultural and restaurant/commercial attractions beside an attractive multilevel promenade along the river. A striking new pedestrian bridge, complete with seating and viewing perches, links the two sides, supplementing the older bridge crossings.

Southgate's main, three-story building houses one hundred tenants. The exterior is covered in a handsome dark-gray basalt, a stone found throughout Melbourne, which is also used for the walkways. Colorful cafe umbrellas, restaurant balconies, banners and public art pieces help enliven the scene. The hard-edged walkway, with several levels, contrasts

PREVIOUS PAGES: **Southgate, left, blends easily into the cityscape of downtown Melbourne, right.**

ABOVE: **One of many sculptures commissioned for the public spaces of Southgate.**

LEFT: **Popular cafe and restaurant decks overlook the Southgate promenade, the Yarra River and downtown Melbourne.**

BELOW LEFT: **The promenade, which runs by restaurants and shops, is enhanced by landscaping and lighting details.**

OPPOSITE: **A seating area in the entrance way is a popular spot on pleasant days.**

72

with the green, natural banks just upriver. Ferries and tour boats dock at the lower level of the promenade, while the upper level is lined with plane trees and has attractive benches, lamp posts and garbage receptacles. The restaurants and cafes are said to be among the most popular destinations for young people in Melbourne.

Southgate's other components are less public and include a four-hundred-room hotel, two office towers, parking and a small church. Apartments have gone up nearby and more units are proposed. The office component is the least successful element, centering on a bleak courtyard, with no public uses at ground level and appearing, at thirteen stories, too tall for the area.

Coming into place downriver, to the west, are a large gambling casino and an exhibition center. A major upgrading of the present Maritime Museum, which is located here, is also planned. Across the river is the even more ambitious Docklands area of more than five hundred acres. Plans of the Docklands Authority call for as many as five thousand residents to be living here by 2005, and still more developments are projected for other sites along the north of the river.

An important question will be whether an attraction such as a casino, with its own restaurants and bars, will draw people away from the pioneering Southgate public precinct, or whether the development will remain a popular destination for even greater numbers of people brought south of the Yarra. Whatever the future holds, in the mid-1990s, Southgate's riverfront successfully presented a new commercial and entertainment focus for the city.

ZUIDERTERRAS CAFE/RESTAURANT

Antwerp,
BELGIUM

project name	Zuiderterras Cafe/Restaurant
water body	River Schelde
size	20.48 x 11.7 x 20.6 meters
completion date	1991
sponsor	NV Zuiderterras
designers	bOb Van Reeth
contact person	bOb Van Reeth
	A.W.G.
	Paardenmarkt 85
	Antwerp B-2000
	Belgium
	Tel. 32 3 233 8470
	Fax 32 3 231 8845

74

BELOW: **The Zuiderterras cafe/restaurant**
punctuates the southern end of the elevated
promenade along the River Schelde.

A splendid site at one end of a promenade beside and above the Schelde River in downtown Antwerp is now fully matched by a well-executed new building. Zuiderterras Cafe not only takes full advantage of its prominent position, it enhances it.

Built in 1991, Zuiderterras replaces a facility that was a counterpart to Noorderterras, a historic restaurant structure at the opposite, northern, end of the promenade. Today they are a distinctive pair of public attractions, one sleek, brown and white, the other traditional brick. In between is a wide, unassuming and welcoming walkway that effectively presents the two restaurants as bookends on the downtown riverfront promenade.

The cafe of Zuiderterras spills onto the promenade with outdoor tables, chairs and windscreen. The restaurant/cafe dominates the second and third levels of the structure; there is a separate bar on another level and offices on top. The main entrance is positioned at mid-level in the building, and below the promenade are the kitchen, delivery ramp and boat tie-ups.

RIGHT: **The view from the bar atop Zuiderterras takes in the active port area below.**

BELOW: **Zuiderterras, on the River Schelde, sits on the end of a promenade deck and next to old marine sheds that are now used for a maritime museum and parking.**

At the south end, a conical tower, about six stories in height, is capped in a distinctive brown color that is used to offset the otherwise white-and-glass building. This tower houses the elevator, but also serves as visual punctuation.

Inside there is wide use of rich, brown wood, tying in the accent color from outside. Floor-to-ceiling windows on the river side of the cafe provide what have to be the best views in the city of the river traffic moving up and down the Schelde. Although the port of Antwerp has moved away from the city center, there is still a substantial amount of activity along the river, including that of pleasure boats. The decor, using black Formica tables, black canvas, dark wood chairs and metal floors, is at once sophisticated and understated, so as not to upstage the river scene. The interior scheme also uses mirrors to good advantage, as these are not large spaces. The mirrors also pick up and reflect the riverside setting so that people seated at all angles can enjoy the view.

Zuiderterras is said to be a very popular meeting spot. Apart from that, it is an exemplary waterfront facility in its orientation to the River Schelde beside it. The project is striking in its modern design but manages at the same time to be warm and welcoming. Vantage points such as this site possesses are special, and in the new Zuiderterras Cafe, Antwerp has a facility that more than measures up.

PREVIOUS PAGES: **Zuiderterras is a small point of contrast with the historic cityscape of downtown Antwerp.**

LEFT: **The mirrored wall, checked tile and porthole window of the ladies room are among the project's striking interior design elements.**

OPPOSITE: **The distintive cylindrical stair tower reflects the vertical elements in the Antwerp skyline.**

RIGHT: **Mezzanine level of the cafe as seen from the bridge to the stair tower.**

BELOW: **Zuiderterras Cafe/Restaurant interiors emphasize dark wood, accented by extensive glass and mirrors, with panoramic views of the river and city.**

QUEEN'S QUAY TERMINAL

Toronto,
Ontario, *CANADA*

project name	Queen's Quay Terminal
water body	Lake Ontario
size	880,000 square feet
cost	$50.5 million
completion date	1983
sponsor	Olympia and York Developments Ltd.
designers	Zeidler Roberts Partnership, Architects
contact person	Eberhard Zeidler
	Zeidler Roberts Partnership, Architects
	315 Queen Street
	West Toronto
	Ontario M5A 1S1
	Canada
	Tel. 1 416 596 8300

Opened in 1927, this massive, eight-story warehouse was soon filled with goods from around the country and the world. Salmon from British Columbia, beef from Argentina, dates from Iraq, butter from New Zealand and manufactured goods from England—as many as 3,600 commodities found their way to this lakefront giant with one million square feet of space.

Ownership of the dockside terminal, near Toronto's central rail yard, changed hands several times over the years until it was finally taken over by the federal government in 1972. This was the first step toward what became known as the Harbourfront project, a federally sponsored make-over of the entire central Toronto waterfront. In 1980 a design competition for the development of the ninety-five-acre centerpiece property was held. Three years later the winning development firm and its architects, both from Toronto, completed a dazzling conversion.

OPPOSITE: **Queen's Quay Terminal, extensively remodeled, retains its Art Deco clock tower from 1927.**

ABOVE: **Queen's Quay Terminal, center, anchors the eastern end of the 92-acre Harbourfront precinct, which is separated from downtown Toronto by an expressway and rail lines.**

Today, the Queen's Quay Terminal, including its signature clock tower at the front, or city, side, is faithful to the Art Deco appearance of the original structure, though floors have been added to the top, opening large spaces inside, and a totally new, glass-enclosed harbor frontage has been constructed. An adjoining cold-storage building was knocked down, allowing views to Lake Ontario from both downtown and the highway that severs Toronto from its lakeside.

The first two floors house shops, restaurants, markets and walkways that lead out to the lake itself. Along one side, to the east, is an arcade that is opened up when the weather is good and enclosed when it is not, so that pedestrians are encouraged to make the walk to the waterfront at anytime of year.

The next six floors house offices as well as a cultural facility that centers on a 450-seat dance theater. Not only is an extensive dance program offered here,

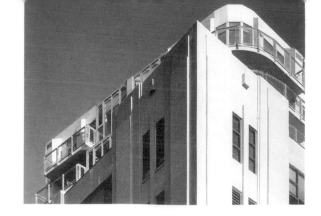

OPPOSITE: **One of three atria that have been
introduced to brighten the interior of the
former warehouse.**

ABOVE: **Atop an old building corner are four
new floors containing 72 condominiums.**

BELOW: **The eastern edge of Queens Quay contains
boat moorings and a glass-enclosed arcade.**

but there are authors' festivals, film screenings and a children's theater taking place. The environment for all of these activities is light and airy, as three atria through the building allow natural light to penetrate past the terraced offices down to the retail spaces. Adding four floors to the structure are seventy-two condominiums in green, glass-enclosed units, each with a sun room and terrace to take advantage of splendid lake and city views.

The most dramatic intervention occurs on the lake side of the terminal. Here the architect cut into a corner of the building and added a glass atrium that runs several floors high and extends along two sides of the building. Slabs of flooring were partially removed to create a sense of openness and a connection from building to lakeside. At the water's edge is a wide, two-level promenade that is well outfitted and enormously popular with strollers and cafe-goers during summer months.

The Harbourfront project has had a controversial history. It received early acclaim, but in the late 1980s it encountered a citizen revolt over certain actions, which led to a shutdown of its property development and a takeover by a new commission. By 1991 all that remained was Harbourfront Centre, a hallmark of the Harbourfront project since its inception, which continues to sponsor a variety of public events.

Through it all the quality of the transformation at Queen's Quay is undiminished, and its popularity continues unabated. An important part of Toronto's industrial heritage has been preserved, albeit in a new guise.

NAVY PIER

Chicago,
Illinois, *USA*

project name	Navy Pier
water body	Lake Michigan
size	3,000 feet (length)
cost	$150 million
completion date	1995
sponsor	Metropolitan Pier and Exposition Authority
designers	Thompson and Wood Associates
contact person	Jane Thompson
	Thompson and Wood Associates
	14 Story Street
	Cambridge, MA 02138
	USA
	Tel. 1 617 349 3600
	Fax 1 617 349 3601

For a number of years there was a debate about what role, if any, Navy Pier should play in the development of the city of Chicago. Over time, it had variously hosted soldiers (during World War I), summer festivals, the Navy, including facilities for pilot training (during World War II), a University of Illinois campus and, lastly, an exhibition center. However, jutting three thousand feet into Lake Michigan, the pier was isolated, and, after a long and colorful history, had become empty and virtually abandoned by 1970.

Salvation came in the late 1970s when Chicago Fest brought millions of visitors to the facility, stimulating a move for the planning and development of a more permanent use for the site. After fits and starts by succeeding municipal administrations, a design competition was held in 1991, from which a scheme by the firm Benjamin Thompson and Associates, of Cambridge, Massachusetts, was chosen. On July 14, 1995, nearly eighty years after it began life as a municipal pier designed to handle river traffic (it sits beside the Chicago River) and to provide recreation (with the Grand Ballroom at the pier end), Navy Pier was reborn.

Now the pier is a giant entertainment facility that provides some of the greatest views available of the Chicago skyline and lakefront. The structure is pleasantly dominated by a Ferris wheel located about one third of the way down the pier. Apparently controversial, the wheel at night is indisputably a major landmark and has historic significance—George Ferris first displayed the amusement ride that now carries his name in Chicago in 1883.

The pier is organized in distinct zones. Behind the retained pier headhouse entrance is what is called the

The Family Pavilion, with children's museum, and six-story Crystal Gardens, was among the first attractions on the newly refurbished Navy Pier on Lake Michigan.

The six-story Crystal Gardens, a one-acre

atrium, houses a wide-ranging botanical display.

Family Pavilion, which includes shops, restaurants, an IMAX theater and a new Children's Museum. Next to that is the Crystal Gardens, a six-story glass atrium containing a giant botanical display, including palm trees from the Southwest, Chinese evergreens and as many as 240 seasonal flowers.

Along the south dock are tour boats, entertainment stages, retail carts and a public walkway, named Dock Street, that stretches the entire length of the pier. Pier Park is next to the south dock and features the Ferris wheel and a new, 1880s-style carousel. Pier Park also features a pond/skating rink. Skyline Stage,

a tensile structure seating 1,500, occupies the middle of the pier, and below it is a level of shops.

At Festival Hall, a new building situated toward the end of the pier, are exposition spaces—for gatherings not large enough to fill Chicago's main exposition center—and meeting rooms. Next there is a beer garden and, finally, the Grand Ballroom, outside of which is an open public space known as the East End. The ballroom's former grandeur, including its eighty-foot domed ceiling, has been restored, and it will be used for special events and performances, much as it was in its early days.

LEFT: **The Crystal Gardens atrium features palm trees from the American Southwest.**

OPPOSITE AND BELOW: **A summer theater tensile structure is a new venue that has been erected atop a shopping arcade.**

CHAPTER 3

The Cultural, Educational and Environmental
Waterfront

From major aquariums, which possess a unique ability to fascinate and educate people about the natural world, to emotionally charged memorials, waterfront cultural and educational sites are among the most engaging features of modern cities. Waterfronts have been providing beautiful settings for religious architecture, memorials, public art and grand cultural institutions for generations, and the practice continues today.

In the late 1950s when Australia wished to signal its coming of age to the postwar world, the glorious Sydney Opera House on Bennalong Point was created. The white, sail-like structure, auspiciously located on the harbor, is a symbol not only for Sydney, but for Australia as a whole. Osaka, Japan, has twin attractions—the Ring of Fire Aquarium and the Suntory Museum—dramatic, bold architectural features prominently positioned on its harbor. Following a different, no less valid, aesthetic, the Monterey Bay Aquarium in Monterey, California, artfully echoes the cannery tradition of that city's waterfront as immortalized in John Steinbeck's *Cannery Row*, which takes place there.

No one can visit the Japanese-American Historic Plaza in Portland, Oregon, and not be moved by the story of the internment of Japanese-Americans during the hysteria of the early days of World War II. Likewise, the starkly simple Holocaust memorial, set in the shadow of the cathedral of Notre Dame in Paris and ingeniously framing a glimpse of the Seine through an iron grate at the tip of the Ile de la Cité, is a stunning piece of public art. Equally moving is the Peace Memorial Park in Hiroshima. (See p. 197.)

Waterfront sites are also logical locations for facilities celebrating maritime heritage. The seafaring history of New Zealand and Sweden come to life in the vessels and memorabilia displayed in the waterfront museums in Auckland and Stockholm, two of the more recent and compelling examples of this type of exhibition (see pp. 203 and 216).

At the root of these and other projects featured in *The New Waterfront* is water cleanup. Massive efforts and large sums of money go along with the commitment to correct years of pollutive practices. The story of Xochimilco in Mexico City is no less amazing than the tale from Santos, Brazil (see p. 194); the one a result of a federal government initiative, the other of a grass-roots, citizen-led effort.

Aside from their aesthetic or symbolic power, many educational and environmental installations inform the public about the world water supply and its influence on our lives. Whether a modern aquarium or modest ecological park, such facilities can reach people of all ages, especially the young, as few others can. The first up-close encounter with an octopus or a sea anemone can be a revelatory experience for almost anyone and leave a lasting impression. The best of the recent cultural, educational and environmental waterfront installations emphasize the vital connections between man and water and can have a real effect on the way we think about this basic resource.

OPPOSITE: **The Hetjens-Film Museum, beside the Rhine River in Düsseldorf, anchors a mixed-use project built around a former harbor basin (see p. 208).**

> *If we can revise our attitudes towards the land under our feet; if we can accept a role of steward and depart from the role of conqueror; if we can accept the view that man and nature are inseparable parts of the unified whole—then Tasmania can be a shining beacon in a dull, uniform and largely artificial world.*
>
> Olegas Truchanas, 1971

See these projects in the Gazetteer:

Mar del Plata Aquarium, Argentina
Japanese American Plaza, Portland, Oregon, USA
S.O.S. Praias, Santos, Brazil
Peace Memorial Garden, Hiroshima, Japan
Tokyo Port Wild Bird Park, Japan
Tokyo Sea Life Park, Japan
Nippon-maru Park, Yokohama, Japan
Salamanca Arts Centre, Hobart, Tasmania, Australia
Bond University, Queensland, Australia
Arnolfini, Bristol, UK
Discovery Point, Dundee, Scotland
Hetjens-Film Museum, Düsseldorf, Germany
Hull Museum of Transportation, UK
Museum Ludwig and Köln Philharmonic,
    Köln/Cologne, Germany
Merseyside Maritime Museum, Liverpool, UK
Camley Street Natural Park, London, UK
Musik- und Kongresshalle, Lübeck, Germany
Aker River Park, Oslo, Norway
Mémorial des Martyrs de la Déportation, Paris, France
Vasa Museum, Stockholm, Sweden
Stockholm Water Festival, Sweden
Sunderland Sculpture Project, UK

89

RING OF FIRE AQUARIUM

Osaka,
JAPAN

project name	Ring of Fire Aquarium
water body	Osaka Bay
size	13,429 square meteres (site)
	3,984 square meters (building)
cost	$107 million
completion date	1990
sponsor	Osaka Waterfront Development Co., Ltd.
designers	Cambridge Seven Associates, Inc.
contact person	Susan Roddy
	Cambridge Seven Associates, Inc.
	1050 Massachusetts Avenue
	Cambridge, MA 02138
	USA
	Tel. 1 617 492 7000
	Fax 1 617 492 7007

Built on a prominent site in Osaka's harbor, the Ring of Fire Aquarium, opened in July 1990, is a powerful public magnet. Before it was redeveloped, the Tempozan district was filled with dilapidated warehouses, but by February 1994 the Aquarium had drawn fifteen million visitors.

The Osaka Aquarium, officially called *Kaiyukan*, is better known as the "Ring of Fire" for its main theme, which focuses on the Pacific Ocean and surrounding

The Ring of Fire Aquarium coexists at a pier end with a cruise-ship loading facility.

LEFT: **The aquarium's courtyard, with support building at right. Colorful tile murals are the work of Ivan Chermayeff.**

BELOW: **The many large, acrylic tanks allow closeup, awe-inspiring views of marine life.**

ring of volcanoes. A central, 1.4 million-gallon tank symbolizes the Pacific and contains a great white shark among a host of other aquatic creatures.

The aquarium is made up of two buildings; the smaller, less dramatically styled, is an entry and support building with an overflow terrace. Visitors ride to the top of the aquarium on a glass-enclosed escalator that allows excellent views of the harbor.

There are eight major and six smaller exhibits of habitats that are arranged along an internal passageway and accompanied by bright graphics and sound effects. The visitor experience is effectively a short course on the distinct environments that make up the Pacific Rim, from Japan's northwestern forest region to Ecuador and Chile, Antarctica and the Tasman Sea.

The aquarium building sits on a vibrant blue base faced with a very colorful tile mosaic depicting marine life. Four large glass and red-tile structures atop the base have a dramatic angular appearance, particularly at night when the interior is illuminated.

Surrounding the twin aquarium buildings is a public promenade and a water-bus dock. A cruise-ship terminal abuts a shopping mall that was built along with the aquarium.

The Osaka aquarium, spanning nearly 300,000 square feet, is the work of Cambridge Seven Associates, of Cambridge, Massachusetts, who are pioneers in aquarium design, having built aquariums in Boston and Baltimore, among other places. Sponsorship is unusual: the Osaka Waterfront Development Co., Ltd. is funded by the City of Osaka and the investment of twenty-seven private firms. The aquarium/shopping mall complex cost $148 million.

With the stellar twin attractions of the Ring of Fire Aquarium and Suntory Museum, Osaka Harbor is well on the way to establishing a new identity within Japan and around the world.

MONTEREY BAY AQUARIUM

Monterey,
California, *USA*

project name	Monterey Bay Aquarium
water body	Monterey Bay
size	216,000 square feet (original)
	93,000 square feet (addition)
cost	$50 million; $28.6 million addition
completion date	1984; 1996 (addition)
sponsor	Monterey Bay Aquarium
designers	Esherick Homsey Dodge and Davis,
	San Francisco
contact person	Jim Heckers
	Monterey Bay Aquarium
	886 Cannery Row
	Monterey CA 93940
	USA
	Tel. 1 408 648 4800

**Dilapidated Cannery Row after the
sardine fishing industry collapsed.**

Opening in October 1984, the Monterey Bay Aquarium was a pacesetter in waterfront development for two reasons. First, its exhibits celebrate the ecosystem of the body of water it borders, Monterey Bay, on the coast of California. Traditionally, aquariums feature exotic species from around the world. Subsequent to the resounding success of Monterey, both from a popular and a scientific research standpoint, other new aquariums have concentrated on the nearby native species and environment, as in Chattanooga, Tennessee, where the emphasis is on the local river ecosystem. The Monterey facility does have temporary exhibits of species from outside the area; for example, a 1992 program featured sharks.

Monterey's second achievement is in setting a standard for contextual architecture. Sited at the end of Cannery Row, where the Hovden sardine cannery operated until 1972, the structure, which is almost entirely new, echoes the look and feel of the industrial facilities that once dominated the waterfront. Restored boilers and smokestacks from the original plant have been incorporated into the design. In addition to the restoration of some of the architecture, the history of the sardine industry is honored in a display of photographs and artifacts .

The Giant Kelp Tank, the featured exhibit, rises two stories and holds 335,000 gallons of water. Behind seven-inch thick clear acrylic walls, the under-

water kelp plant native to the coast grows gracefully, and schools of anchovies are fed daily by divers.

Another, smaller, tank holds a sea otter exhibit, which is a popular attraction. This threatened marine mammal is the subject of a research effort at the aquarium that entails a tagging program of as many as sixty wild otters since 1985 and a care program for orphaned sea otter pups.

A Great Tide Pool, formed by the wings of the structure, juts into the bay and is an open-air exhibit where daily tides wash in and out. A variety of animals reside here, with visitors enjoying an up-close view. In another location, a screened area is home to shore birds and plants.

As many as six hundred volunteers donate time to the aquarium (after first being trained by the facility's educational staff). Free school tours and classes are offered, and programs for teachers are available. Attendance is at two million a year, and enough revenue is being generated to support an addition that will cost another $30 million.

Sponsorship of the aquarium is unusual. Whereas most major aquariums are government sponsored or operate as businesses, a $50-million private gift underwrote the Monterey Bay project. Planned for opening in 1996, a new wing will feature the mysteries of the deep sea and the open ocean outside the bay.

TOP: **Fiberglass models of whales and other marine mammals are featured.**

ABOVE: **An aerial view shows the aquarium's orientation toward Monterey Bay, on which its educational exhibits and research efforts are concentrated. Decks overlook a tidal pool.**

SUNTORY MUSEUM

Osaka,
JAPAN

project name	Suntory Museum
water body	Osaka Bay
size	13,429 square meters (site)
	3,984 square meters (building)
cost	12 billion yen
completion date	1994
sponsor	Osaka Waterfront Developments
designers	Tadao Ando Architect Associates
contact person	Koji Morita
	Suntory Museum
	1-5-10 Kaigan-dori Minato-ku
	Osaka 552
	JAPAN
	Tel. 81 6 577 0001 Fax 81 6 577 9200

In the fall of 1994, a stunning installation, the Suntory Museum, was completed on a harbor site that had already been made popular by the new Ring of Fire Aquarium immediately adjoining.

Standing alone, the Suntory Museum would be a major institution and a significant public attraction. By locating two such strong buildings side-by-side where there is also a "festival marketplace" shopping mall, Osaka clearly aims to transform some of its vast waterfront for intense public use.

More remarkable than the pairing of two major facilities is the fact that, despite being designed by

OPPOSITE: **The Suntory Museum's distinctive round glass form, right, contrasts with the angular glass top of the Ring of Fire Aquarium.**

ABOVE: **A wide plaza stretches 100 meters along the harbor's edge.**

LEFT: **The inverted cone contains an IMAX theater in a circular structure behind the glass curtain wall; the building at right contains gallery spaces.**

The Suntory Museum emphasizes its water orientation with a stepped plaza and waterside public art.

completely different firms—one American, the other Japanese—and having dissimilar appearances, the aquarium and museum fit well together. Both strive to take advantage of the harbor location, with wide public plazas facing the west, and both signal the coming of age of Osaka, a city traditionally known as Japan's gray, industrial metropolis.

Whereas most facilities housing IMAX or similar functions are interior-looking boxes, the Suntory Museum, which opened in November 1994, manages to house a huge IMAX theater as well as gallery space in a structure that still focuses on the harbor.

The dominant shape in architect Tadao Ando's design is an inverted cone that contains the theater (and a screen that measures 20 x 28 meters). A glass curtain wall faces the harbor, and two glass-walled rectangular structures overlook a large promenade and steps to the water's edge. One of these structures houses a restaurant that offers spectacular harbor views from the second story. The other block contains a gallery with two levels of exhibit space. On the top, ninth, floor of the museum is a Sky Lounge.

The Suntory Museum, which cost about 12 billion yen to build, contains 12,400 square meters of space. The second phase of the remake of the Tempozan district, consisting of a movie theater, museum, restaurant and hotel, will cost $160 million and was still under construction as of spring 1996.

LEFT: **Looking west, five pillars at the water's edge are repeated on a breakwater 70 meters from the shore.**

TOP RIGHT AND BELOW: **The large plaza with its sculptural forms overlooks the cranes of the Port of Osaka.**

TOP LEFT AND BELOW: **A harborside view takes in the contrasting shapes of the principal museum structures, IMAX theater, plaza and art pieces.**

XOCHIMILCO ECOLOGICAL PARK

Mexico City,
MEXICO

project name	Parque Ecológico Xochimilco
water body	Lake Huetzalin
size	7,400 acres (project); 660 acres (park)
completion date	1993
sponsor	The Federal District of Mexico City and Delegación Xochimilco
designers	Grupo de Diseño Urbano, S.C.
contact person	Mario Schjetnan-Jose Luis Perez
	Grupo de Diseño Urbano, S.C.
	Fernando Montes de Oca No.4
	Col. Conesa
	Mexico City 06140
	Mexico
	Tel. 52 5 553 1248 Fax 52 5 286 1013

Colorful boats lining the shore take visitors onto Lago Xochilita and into restored ancient farming areas.

The vast metropolis that is Mexico City was once an island outpost amid a huge system of interconnected lakes. Even in 1850, the burgeoning city still had five large lakes to the north, east and south.

Vestiges of three still exist today—Zumpango well to the north, Texcoco on the east and Xochimilco to the south. In the case of Xochimilco, the combination of pollution, urban crowding and underground aquifer depletion had produced a severely degraded water body.

The site of productive farming for centuries, Xochimilco was gradually abandoned. The pre-Hispanic system of agriculture known as the *chinampas*, where lake-bottom mud was piled on reeds to make farmland that was stabilized by willow trees whose roots held back the canal water, was in danger of disappearing. Pollution, siltation, weeds and encroaching urban settlement all contributed to the problem.

A favorite outing spot, where colorful boats once glided through the canals, Lake Xochimilco has a particularly strong place in the minds and hearts of Mexico City residents. Its historical and cultural importance made Xochimilco a prime target for a cleanup campaign.

Declared a "world inheritance site" in 1987 by UNESCO, Xochimilco was also chosen by former President Salinas for a thorough ecological rescue. The multifaceted master plan involved such actions as flood protection, enhancement of the aquifer, land subsidence prevention, control of land use and development in sensitive areas, the opening of new areas for recreation, construction of substantial new water-

treatment facilities and the reduction of erosion and waste and sewage dumping from nearby hills.

The restoration of and cleansing of the area have meant the return of farming and recreation activities. Furthermore, there are places within Parque Ecológico Xochimilco where you can look out over the water, see the sacred mountain ranges in the distance, and for a moment experience a living, historical landscape. (To enhance the views, electrical wires were consolidated and relocated.)

The focal point for the entire project is the Ecological Park, a 660-acre corner of the site that is readily accessible by road. A striking cobalt blue educational and visitor information center is the main architectural feature. A curved, trellised walkway, Paseo del Flores, connects to a lagoon. The building

ABOVE LEFT: **The conical-shaped tower, upper right, was modeled on an ancient pumping device and marks the visitors' information center and entrance to the Ecological Park.**

TOP: **The semicircular structure anchoring the boat landing echoes the shape of the visitors' center.**

ABOVE: **An aerial view of the stalls that make up the vast flower market.**

PERVIOUS PAGES: **The colorful visitors' center on Lake Huetzalin is the dominant structure in Xochimilco Ecological Park.**

ABOVE: **The Paseo de las Flores is bordered with experimental plantings.**

RIGHT: **The plant and flower market contains 1,700 vendors in greenhouse-like stalls.**

BELOW: **A circular patio atop the visitors' center allows for views of the entire park and, through the skylight, into the museum below.**

is surrounded by flowers and planted ground cover. The interior is bathed in deep reds, purples and blues. A round pool at the center is positioned beneath an open skylight.

Other major components of the park include a large sports area with baseball and football fields and courts for volleyball, basketball, handball, softball and tennis. Another area contains a plant and flower market with 1,700 stalls—the major source for the city.

The project covers an immense 7,400 acres, including 200 kilometers of canals and lagoons and 2,700 acres of restored agricultural lands. Undertaken from 1989 to 1993 by various agencies of the Mexico City government and the borough of Xochimilco, the restoration is a triumph, both from an ecological standpoint and as urban design.

LEFT: **A pedestrian bridge leads to a path around Lake Acitlalin.**

RIGHT: **A terraced plaza adjoins the visitors' center next to the Paseo de las Flores, left.**

BELOW: **The pumping system that maintains the water quality is housed in structures that jut into the lagoon.**

BELOW RIGHT: **A sculpture of an ancient pump was modeled on Archimedes' screw.**

MIKAELI CONCERT AND CONFERENCE HALL

Mikkeli,
FINLAND

project name	Mikaeli Concert and Congress Hall
water body	Lake Pankalampi
size	5,300 square meters
completion date	1988
sponsor	City of Mikkeli
designers	Arkkitehitoimisto Arto Sipinen Oy
contact person	Arto Sipinen SAFA
	Arto Sipinen
	Ahertajantie 3
	Espoo 02100
	Finland
	Tel. 358 0 455 2011
	Fax 358 0 455 2513

TOP: **The Mikaeli Concert and Congress**
(conference) Hall. Poles at left mark a path
to the landscaped parking area.

ABOVE: **The cafeteria is housed behind the curved**
glass wall, left. The large concert hall is at right.

LEFT: **The simplicity of the design complements**
the park-like setting on Lake Pankalampi.

This exquisite concert hall sits on the outskirts of the city of Mikkeli on axis with the cathedral and railway station, previously the most dominant features of the cityscape, and forms a prominent new western anchor for Mikkeli.

The site beside Lake Pankalampi figures significantly in the hall's design. Large expanses of glass, including an undulating glass wall in the cafe, provide panoramic vistas. The lake is reflected against the walls on the outside, and the interiors are in muted tones to correspond with the natural setting. Overall, the building has an atmosphere of calm and repose, encouraging a mood of contemplation that is accentuated by the lakeside setting.

The main concert hall has 694 seats, 172 in the gallery. The structure also houses a chamber music hall with 166 seats. The acoustic design, the work of Alpo Holme, is said to be one of the best in Europe. The concert hall currently displays works of modern art—paintings and sculpture. The same spaces are used for conferences.

The Mikaeli Concert and Congress (conference) Hall was built on the occasion of the 150th anniversary of the city of Mikkeli, which administers the facility, and was designed by Arto Sipinen, an architect working in the tradition of Alvar Aalto.

A night view reveals the relationship of the main concert hall, right, with the small hall, seating 166, behind the cafeteria at left.

ABOVE: **The stage of Martti Talvela Hall.**

RIGHT: **The glass walls of the main concert hall
entrance provide uninterrupted views of the
cafeteria wing, lake and surrounding woodland.**

BELOW: **The main concert hall seats 694 on the
principal level, 172 in the gallery.**

GRONINGER MUSEUM

Groningen,
THE NETHERLANDS

project name	Groninger Museum
water body	Verbindings Canal
size	8,050 square meters
cost	DFl. 57.5 million
completion date	1994
sponsor	Groninger Museum and Dept. of City Planning
designers	Alessandro Mendini (master plan)
contact person	Jeanine de Boer
	Groninger Museum
	Museumeiland 1
	Groningen 9711 ME
	The Netherlands
	Tel. 31 50 3 666 555
	Fax 31 50 3 120 815

Occupying a historic place on Groningen's inner harbor, along the Verbindings Canal, is the strikingly contemporary Groninger Museum of Art. A pedestrian bridge that is integrated into the museum connects the train station with the historic center, so that the Groninger acts as a new gateway to the city as well a symbol of Groningen's association with the arts.

The museum's exhibits are wide-ranging, from traditional Dutch paintings and crafts to contemporary art, film and work that crosses disciplines, such as crafts designed by architects. There is also an archaeological collection and exhibits on the early history of Groningen.

The principal architect, Alessandro Mendini of Milan, chose to make four separate buildings that are connected by corridors, and enlisted three guest architects to design the individual components. Thus,

at the western end there is a circular aluminum gallery housing the applied arts collection, which is displayed in an illuminated showcase that encircles the room. In the floor is an installation representing the bottom of the South China Sea, where part of the museum's collection of Oriental ceramics was found. Below this gallery is a square brick structure that contains the Groningen history collection and archaeology exhibits.

The dominant structure is a thirty-meter-tall tower, clad in gold-colored laminate, in which the museum's permanent collection is stored. Rather than burying the repository, as many museums do, the architect wanted to put the material in a building that makes a statement. Temporary exhibits are housed in a space beside the tower, where there are also offices, a shop, a cafe and an auditorium.

The Groninger Museum, with its distinctive gold-clad tower, is a new point of entry into Groningen.

TOP: **The circular, aluminum-clad gallery in the foreground houses an applied arts collection.**

LEFT: **Detail of the pavilion for visual arts, which features a roof of red steel plates.**

RIGHT: **Spiral staircase in the Mendini Pavilion, which houses a visual arts collection that dates from 1500.**

The most fantastic component of the Groninger Museum is the pavilion for visual arts, with two floors covered in a bright, multicolored laminate. Modern visual material is displayed here. Atop this space is a structure that has a roof made of unconnected red steel plates and houses the Old Visual Arts collection, which dates from 1500 to 1950.

The Groninger Museum is a bold presence on the city's principal canal. Incorporating unusual perspectives of the waterfront, it stands in dramatic contrast to Groningen's traditional architecture.

STRAHAN WHARF CENTRE

Strahan,
Tasmania, AUSTRALIA

project name	Strahan Wharf Centre
water body	Macquarie Harbour
cost	Aus. $1 million
completion date	1992
sponsor	Strahan Wharf Centre
designers	Robert Morris-Nunn
contact person	Bill Mabey
	Strahan Wharf Centre
	The Esplanade
	P.O. Box 73
	Strahan, Tasmania 7468
	Australia
	Tel. 61 04 71 7488
	Fax 61 04 71 7461

On the dockside of the small community of Strahan, on the western coast of Tasmania, is an unprepossessing structure built of corrugated tin and huge logs, its eclectic, shed-like appearance reflecting the boat-building and timber-milling heritage of the town. The Strahan Wharf Centre is a highly unusual educational and cultural facility whose lobby area does double duty as a standard visitors' center, with basic tourist information and a small bookshop at one end and, at the other, a sailor's memorial etched on a glass window that faces the harbor.

The interpretive museum is divided into several small, intimate areas beneath a high ceiling. Visitors are led through an evocative historical and ecological tour. Most of the senses are engaged: smells of decaying peat, the feel of rain-forest humidity, the touch of native pine from the forests that provided the country's first export. Throughout there is the sound of water falling and views of the bay are ever present through the glass wall. Both artist and botanist have left their imprint here.

A pebbled path lined with natural greenery guides visitors through exhibits that touch on aboriginal issues and national history, and a short climb up a rocky path lets you peer into the cabin of a "piner." The heritage of the pine industry is told through historic photos and artifacts. There are also exhibits on hydro-power, the railroad and environmental struggles. Videos and illustrations are used for imaginative displays.

The approach of the Centre is very low-key. Strahan is also the jumping-off point for people on their way to explore the preserved forest areas, and the organizers are content to raise curiosity and interest rather than attempt a definitive interpretation of the area's ecology or history.

However, in symbolism and impact, Strahan Centre is much larger and more important than its modest outward appearance suggests. The multifaceted experience documents and celebrates the coming of age of the environmental movement not only in Tasmania, but throughout Australia. As the largest accessible community in the western part of the state, Strahan became the rallying point for protesters against planned dams and logging operations that endangered the rain forest.

LEFT: **The main entrance to Strahan Wharf Centre serves as a tourist information facility as well as a cultural and historical museum.**

RIGHT: **A sculpture of a "piner" is part of a display about the area's pine-logging history.**

RIGHT: **A detail of the center's glass-canopy and pole-supported roof.**

BELOW: **A floor-to-ceiling glass wall facing Macquarie Harbour allows natural light into the museum and waterfront views.**

BELOW RIGHT: **Pine beams, integral to the natural and cultural heritage of northwest Tasmania, clad the exterior.**

111

The effort of residents and their allies to protect this natural resource led to significant portions being set aside as World Heritage Area and national park. Additional areas are applying for protection.

Though the Wharf Centre has succeeded in acquainting the visitor with Strahan's rich environmental heritage, one of the frustrations is that cruise ships drop visitors who stay only fifty minutes. The hope is that the Centre will prove engaging enough to encourage visitors to stay overnight.

The Centre cost an estimated Aus. $1 million, half of which was spent on the building, the other half on the interpretive material.

SYDNEY OPERA HOUSE

Sydney, AUSTRALIA

project name	Sydney Opera House
water body	Sydney Harbour
size	site 5.5 acres; three halls, 4,781 seats
cost	$102 million
completion date	1973
sponsor	Sydney Opera House
designers	Jørn Utzon
contact person	General Manager
	Sydney Opera House
	GPO Box 4274
	Sydney NSW 2001
	Australia
	Tel. 61 2 250 7111
	Fax 61 2 221 8072

BELOW: **The pioneering design of the distinctive roofs of the Sydney Opera House called for pre-cast concrete sections, covered in tiles.**

BOTTOM: **A classic waterfront vista of the the city's principal icons: the Opera House framed by Sydney Harbour Bridge.**

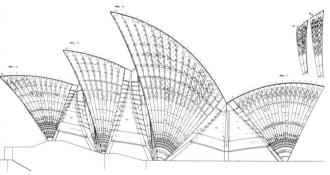

The Sydney Opera House is one of the most memorable waterfront structures in the world. Perhaps the Statue of Liberty in New York Harbor, the Houses of Parliament on the Thames or the statue on Corcovado overlooking the harbor of Rio de Janeiro are comparably vivid urban waterfront images.

Few buildings anywhere have a history as filled with controversy as this opera house, or reflect so dogged a determination in the face of opposition to build something truly magnificent. Even fewer are as well received upon completion and as readily adopted as a national as well as a local symbol.

The story of the opera house begins with the arrival in Australia of Eugene Goosens, who came from England in 1947 to conduct the Australian Broadcasting Commission's Sydney orchestra and called attention to the city's lack of a suitable performance venue. Charles Moses, commission chairman, also became an influential advocate of a new building, and together they captured the imagination and support of the labour premier of New South Wales, Joe Cahill.

The idea of an opera house caught on because it suggested a coming of age of a young, heretofore materialistic city and implied a sophistication that would enhance Sydney's international stature. After a committee had examined thirty sites, it selected Bennalong Point, a peninsula jutting into Sydney Harbour close to the central business district. Named after an Aboriginal that early settlers selected to help "civilize" his people (Bennalong was an English approximation of his name), the location boasted only a tram shed, the proverbial end of the line.

An international design competition was announced in 1955, and the guidelines specified a main hall for up to 3,500 people and a smaller hall for less than half that number. There were 233 entries, which were judged by a team that included two American architects and two architectural professors, one from Sydney and the other from the UK.

Legend has it that Finnish architect Eero Saarinen, who arrived late to the judging, chose the dazzling sketches by Danish architect Jørn Utzon, whose concept the other jurors had discarded, and successfully lobbied for its eventual adoption. However, not only were his bold drawings vague, it became known that the thirty-eight-year-old Utzon had built only two commissions, both of which were housing projects!

Furthermore, Utzon had never been to Sydney. Yet he grasped the site's significance and wrote later about how the diagrams and maps had inspired him. He located foyers at the front, for the harbor views, explaining that "I wanted people to be entertained not only by what they saw in the theaters, but by the spectacular views at interval … "[1] As for the dramatic building shape, it seems obvious that he had sail imagery in mind, although he denied that inspiration.

Joe Cahill decided to finance the construction through a lottery. He announced a deliberately low estimate of Aus. $7 million, which later came to haunt the project as costs escalated to Aus. $102 million. Cahill also pushed for construction to begin before detailed drawings were complete, and the foundation was laid in March 1959. Cahill died before the end of the year, and the opposition voices became stronger.

cafes and shops along the perimeter, and events such as Sunday jazz concerts attract a broad audience. Foyers and balconies provide still more vantage points from which to view the harbor.

Within the three buildings are four stages. The white roof tiles are a remarkable feature; very few of the one million or so used have had to be replaced in more than twenty years. They are the glistening white that Utzon envisioned at the very beginning, reflecting both the sky and the harbor and creating a spectacular presence on Bennalong Point.

Many have denigrated the role of Utzon. Learned tomes have emphasized the cost overrun and engineering complexity; however, *The Sydney Morning Herald*, March 23, 1995, gave a different summary:

Our image (and the world's image too) of Sydney as a beautiful, progressive, free-spirited city has been created, in part at least, by Mr. Utzon's inspired design… The Sydney of the 2000 Olympics is unthinkable without Mr. Utzon's Opera House, which has become a metaphor for the city's vibrant style and culture.

Utzon meanwhile labored in Denmark until moving to Sydney in 1963, while the difficulties of translating his radical design into working drawings grew more complicated, and the engineers became increasingly frustrated. In 1965, the labour party government was overturned and the new public works minister essentially drove Utzon away. Utzon resigned in February 1966, while a main roof of the building was being erected, and never returned to see the result of his vision.

Sir Ove Arup, founder of the engineering company bearing his name, stayed on the job, and Australian architects E. H. Farmer, Peter Hall and Lionel Todd were named to carry on with the project. With many permutations (the roofs went through twelve designs), the new team carried out the essence of Utzon's original concept on the outside but scuttled his interior plans. The latter step is still controversial. The dedication ceremony, which Utzon boycotted, took place in October 1973, sixteen years after the project was originally commissioned.

The resulting Sydney Opera House is really three separate buildings, each with a soaring, white-tiled roof, atop a pod that contains parking space. The building's popularity owes much to its very public nature—it is surrounded by a promenade that offers some of the best harbor views in Sydney. There are

LEFT: **A view across Sydney Cove from a pedestrian walkway that rings the central waterfront.**

BELOW: **A closeup of a roof peak shows some of the 1, 056,000 tiles employed.**

BELOW: **The Opera House, perched dramatically on Bennalong Point, stands out as a national symbol.**

CHAPTER 4

The Historic
Waterfront

Traditionally waterfronts are among the most colorful, and dangerous, areas in a city. Instead of condemning old waterfront structures to non-use, decay and ultimate abandonment, some cities are working toward the preservation and adaptive reuse of historic buildings and precincts, favoring a restorative approach that, in the end, makes for a richer community.

Some commentators complain about gentrification and the creation of false historicity. However, if it were not for the popular appeal of such historic sites and the revenue they generate, which often pays for restoration and upkeep, most historic buildings would fall victim to the wrecking ball and disappear altogether. While an old warehouse reborn as a trendy wine bar is not a "real" warehouse, the reused structure maintains a tangible sense of the past that no new building can. Often the new uses introduced in abandoned buildings—for example, in Exeter, UK (see p. 208)—bring with them a renewed vitality to central city neighborhoods.

An excellent example of a historic waterfront precinct that has been successfully restored is The Rocks in Sydney, where the settlement of Australia began. In spite of the rich history, a redevelopment scheme in the 1960s, which was typical for the time, would have leveled the area and replaced the old, and in many cases deteriorating, structures with modern offices and apartments. Fortunately, the march of new office and apartment towers from the central business district toward the Rocks was halted, and most of the historic buildings, including Sydney's oldest, have now been refurbished. The Rocks now combines rich new architecture and historic buildings with a cluster of boutiques, pubs, restaurants, hotels, houses and offices in one of Sydney's liveliest areas, drawing residents and tourists alike.

Puerto Madero in Buenos Aires, Argentina, is another striking example of a historic waterfront retained, refurbished and brought back to life. In this case, a large former port facility at the foot of the central business district is being converted into a mixed-use precinct. Sixteen old brick warehouses fronting four large basins are being handsomely restored to house offices, condominiums, restaurants and a college campus and administrative facility, with a wide waterside promenade. Obsolete cranes have been retained throughout the site as artifacts of the area's industrial past. Puerto Madero shows every promise of becoming a popular spot in a city with no shortage of entertainment and restaurant venues.

In a similar transformation, pubs, outdoor cafes, restaurants, and artisans' workshops have taken over old sandstone warehouses along the waterfront in Hobart, Tasmania (see p. 203). The area at night still evokes a somewhat haunting feel, recalling the days in the early nineteenth century when Hobart was the departure point for notorious island prisons.

The core section of the ambitious Victoria & Alfred waterfront project in Cape Town, South Africa (see pp. 56–7), is a historic restoration combined with a working dock that has been retained and refurbished. Thus, the city has preserved a historical link, while fulfilling its current commercial needs.

Historic waterfronts are integral to maritime heritage, and as such are usually tied to a city's early prosperity and economic development. Cities that are capable of preserving their historic waterfront districts have the chance to capture the allure that comes from being in touch with the past in modern daily life.

> *…and he kept a part of the old pier in use.*
> Gabriel García Márquez, *Chronicle of a Death Foretold*, 1982

OPPOSITE: **A 5.6-mile canalway ultimately will connect the core of the restored Lowell, Massachusetts, mill district (see p. 191). A path along the Pawtucket Canal is at right.**

See these projects in the Gazetteer:

S.S. Elissa, Galveston, USA
Historic Properties, Halifax, Canada
Heritage Park, Lowell, USA
Le Vieux Port de Montreal, Canada
Ellis Island, New York, USA
Station Square, Pittsburgh, USA
Lake Union Steam Plant, Seattle, USA
Auckland Ferry Building, New Zealand
Dry Dock Museum, Cádiz, Spain
Gloucester Docks, UK
Castlefield Park, Manchester, UK

THE FORKS RENEWAL AND ASSINIBOINE RIVERWALK

Winnipeg,
Manitoba, *CANADA*

project name	Forks Renewal and Assiniboine Riverwalk
water body	Assiniboine River
size	56 acres
cost	Cdn. $32 million
completion date	1987–
sponsor	Forks Renewal Corporation
designers	Cohlmeyer Hanson and Associates, Winnipeg
contact person	Nick Diakiw
	The Forks Renewal Corp.
	404 One Wesley Avenue
	Winnipeg, Manitoba R3C 4C6
	Canada
	Tel. 1 204 943 7752
	Fax 1 204 943 7915

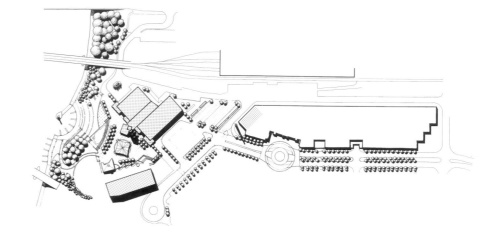

ABOVE: **Site plan. A new one-mile walkway along the Assiniboine River, left, connects the Forks area (shaded) with parliament.**

LEFT: **The Forks Renewal area in summer. Restored railroad buildings, left, house a lively recreation/shopping/eating complex close to downtown Winnipeg.**

The history of Winnipeg, the oldest city in Western Canada, is inextricably bound up with its rivers and its railroads. Those elements are combined in the Forks Renewal project, where, at the site of the first settlement on the juncture of the Red River and the Assiniboine, sixty acres of land became available for redevelopment .

The rivers were the principal reason for the settlement in 1738, and the construction of the Canadian Pacific Railway through the area in the 1880s led to a boom. By the early part of the twentieth century, Winnipeg had developed into a major grain center and had become Canada's third largest city.

For one hundred years, the site at the juncture of the Red and Assiniboine Rivers had been a rail yard and cement plant, and the public had been denied access to this area. In 1987, after years of planning and debate, the land was turned over by the railroad to the Forks Renewal Corporation, a quasi-independent body.

ABOVE: **Site plan with Market buildings lower left, tensile structure center, the Pavilion warming hut above it and restored Johnson Terminal at top.**

LEFT: **Market Plaza. A skating rink/performance area is located under a tensile structure that covers 5,000 square feet.**

BELOW: **The sculptural lighthouse, foreground, marks a semicircular dock. The glass-enclosed observation tower, left, provides panoramic views.**

Before any restoration or development occurred, the first action taken was the establishment of the Forks National Historic Site. A modest structure and play area, as well as walkways and plantings along the Red River, mark these nine acres.

In the mixed-use project that has grown in the remaining space is a collection of historic structures, new construction and recreational space focused on a circular amphitheater that faces the juncture of the rivers. The signature building is a lighthouse on the Assiniboine.

The first significant project was the setting up of a public market in two renovated and expanded turn-of-the-century railroad buildings. The Forks Market comprises a lively mixture of shops and restaurants on two levels and features a five-story glass tower with an elevator that ascends to a platform that offers panoramic views. A plaza lies between the market and the restored Johnson Terminal structure, which houses shops and offices. Dominating the plaza is a tensile structure that shelters an ice-skating rink. To one side is a warming hut.

There are river walkways, including a "Walk through Time" with plaques detailing the city's history and noting the recorded flood levels. The steps leading to the river, built with the inevitable spring floods in mind, are designed to withstand water and ice.

There is a small marina, an archeological site, a section of prairie grass, parking lots and there are plans for additional development. Nearby, a new children's museum occupies a restored building. The Forks has proved surprisingly popular, attracting an estimated five million people a year.

Building on this success, the city undertook a one-mile walkway at the edge of the Assiniboine that connects the Forks with the provincial legislature building. Its sixteen-foot width and careful detailing have made it a much-visited addition. In connection with the walkway was the companion restoration of nearby Bonnycastle Regional Park, both projects being completed at a cost of $5 million.

THE DOCKS

Marseille,
FRANCE

project name	The Docks
water body	Mediterranean Sea
size	100,000 square meters
cost	FFr. 500 million
completion date	1998–
sponsor	SARI
designers	Eric Castaldi Architecte DPLG
contact person	Erick Zerbib, Eric Castaldi Architecte
	10 Place de la Joliette
	Marseille 13304
	France
	Tel. 33 9 190 0283
	Fax 33 9 190 0228

Interior of the 19th-century warehouse showing

old stone walls and beams before restoration.

In the mid-nineteenth century, Marseille was home to one of the world's largest ports, linking Europe with the far reaches of the globe. In 1869, that link was extended, as the Suez Canal provided direct access to the Mediterranean Sea.

The Docks is an immense warehouse complex built at the peak of the ascendancy of the Port of Marseille. Opened in 1863, it measures 365 meters in length, with a total developed area of 80,000 square meters. The Docks comprises 13 seven-story structures that are strung together along an immense block fronting the still-active piers of the port.

Constructed of massive stone and brick, with cast-iron braces, the warehouses fell into disuse like their counterparts around the world as port technology shifted after World War II. The development company SARI acquired the entire complex in 1991 and has begun its gradual rehabilitation into offices, shops and gallery space. The first several segments, beginning at the eastern end at the Place de la Joliette, near the classic Old Port of Marseille, were completed and rented by 1995.

Architect Eric Castaldi has fashioned a respectful intervention. In the central part of each structure an atrium traversed by walkways lets in light from the seventh to the third floors, and additional natural light pours in through interior courtyards. The results are handsome interior spaces that are bathed in sunlight

A reflecting pool is a subtle design feature inside the Docks and is used as exhibition space.

119

The window replacements in the restored stone façade remain faithful to the original.

and an openness that is entirely unexpected when viewing the solid structure from the outside.

On the ground level of the first rehabilitated building, a reflecting pool captures the light cascading down the stone walls, the water almost giving the impression that the building is on a basin, thus evoking its maritime origins. This area is well utilized as an exhibit space.

During development, eight thousand square meters of office space are coming onto the market at one time. The first segment was completely occupied by 1995, and the second segment was half committed by autumn of 1994. A restaurant and cafe will join a travel agency on the ground floor. The plan is to complete the rehabilitation, moving structure by structure, by 1998.

The Docks project is a triumph of adaptive reuse that has ensured that an important historic feature of the Port of Marseille, a handsome series of buildings, has been carefully and thoughtfully maintained for continued use in years to come.

OPPOSITE: **Sunlight from an overhead skylight bathes the interior pool with light and brightens the corridors and offices above.**

BELOW: **Part of the walkway system on the upper levels. The skylight illuminates the spaces below.**

BOAT QUAY

SINGAPORE

project name	Riverfront Conversion, Boat Quay
water body	Singapore River
completion date	1987
sponsor	Urban Redevelopment Authority
contact person	Mrs. Teh Lai Yip
	Urban Redevelopment Authority
	45 Maxwell Road 0106
	Singapore
	Tel. 65 321 8020
	Fax 65 323 4793

Even for a city-state as efficiently run as Singapore, the pronouncement on February 27, 1977, by Prime Minister Lee Kuan Yew, that there was to be fishing in the heavily polluted Singapore River in ten years was startling.

For over a century, residents, businesses and industry alike had treated the island's waterways as dumps and sewers. Cleaning up the Singapore River would not be simply a matter of building sewer lines – the watershed of the Singapore River covered thirty percent of the island. Moreover, any change to the existing system would involve a monumental task of human engineering; for street hawkers, pig farms, over-crowded (and some illegal) shophouses (shops with housing above them) and squatters along the river were all part of the problem.

Seeing the river today, and the restored three- and four-story shophouses of Boat Quay lining the curved section of the river just before it empties into Marina Bay at the heart of the fast-developing downtown, it is hard to imagine it in the 1980s when the river was thoroughly polluted, foul-smelling and filled with trash and the shophouses a shambles. This scene was set against the background of developing office towers that are now the symbol of Singapore's emergence as a vibrant Asian economy.

The twin desires for clean water and some retained sense of traditional Singapore combined to bring about the development of Boat Quay. Of the two efforts, the preservation action is perhaps the more remarkable. Clean water could be seen as a requisite for any modern city-state. But old, outmoded structures, like the river shophouses, could easily have

Boat Quay, a restored section of three- and four-story shophouses along the Singapore River, contrasts with new skyscrapers.

BELOW: **The lighted promenade of Boat Quay, with its many bars and restaurants, is popular with local office workers and visitors alike.**

given way to new office towers. Instead, there developed the recognition that Singapore's rich past had to be preserved, at least in part, and this argument was aided by the prospect of tourist interest.

With the political support of the prime minister, the complicated issues of water cleanup were tackled almost immediately after his 1977 speech. To be on the safe side, the ministers in charge gave themselves an eight-year deadline, allowing a little room for contingencies.

Just relocating the squatters that lined the river was a complicated, time-consuming effort. If they were not Singaporeans, they were not entitled to

resettlement benefits, and there was a danger that they would be forced out on to the streets. Gradually, the squatters were resettled, and non-citizens were allowed to rent flats.

There was also the matter of the pig and duck farms, whose effluent in the past had simply been dumped into the upper reaches of the Singapore River or a tributary. There were 610 pig farms alone, and the ruling that they had to leave Singapore, of course, displaced a number of farmers.

In all, the water cleanup effort brought about the resettlement of 26,000 families from substandard housing, the relocation of 5,000 street hawkers into

ABOVE RIGHT: **Lights from Boat Quay attractions are reflected in the Singapore River.**

LEFT: **This section of the Singapore River was once crowded with hundreds of "bumboats" and squatters in adjoining shophouses.**

BELOW: **Cafes and restaurants at the river's edge provide outdoor dining.**

food centers and the removal of 2,800 river industries. [1]

The last major action was the clearing away of the small wooden boats, called "bumboats," that lined the riverfront. In September 1983, eight hundred were moved down the river to a new anchorage, marking the end of a tradition that went back 160 years. The act troubled many residents and resistance was voiced. (There is a suggestion now that some of the boats may return to the river; the only craft there in 1995 were a few tour boats.) The repair and strengthening of the river walls was undertaken after the bumboats left.

The restoration of the shophouses was carried out by private owners under the leadership of the Urban Redevelopment Authority (URA). The Boat Quay redevelopment program itself dates from 1985, when the cleanup program neared completion. URA's plans also included putting the Clarke Quay area (see p. 201) and an additional riverfront area up for development.

Office workers from the towers now make their way to the landscaped promenade passing by shops, bars and restaurants that line the lower reach of the Singapore River. The restored historic houses feature a variety of architectural styles, which adds a diverse character to the promenade walk.

There is a tangible vitality here both day and night, as Boat Quay has proved a popular tourist attraction as well as a magnet for the Singaporeans.

125

NORRKÖPING INDUSTRIAL LANDSCAPE AND LOUIS DE GEER CONCERT HALL AND CONFERENCE CENTER

Norrköping,
SWEDEN

project name	Norrköping Industrial Landscape/Louis de Geer Concert and Congress Hall
water body	restored loop of the Motala River
size	4,000 square meters
cost	$7 million+
completion date	1993
sponsor	Holmenbyggarna (developer)
designers	FFNS Landskap
contact person	Thhorhjoorn Anderson
	Engelbrektsplan 1
	Box 5503
	Stockholm 114 85
	Sweden
	Tel. 46 8 700 3000
	Fax 46 8 700 3100

The Louis De Geer Concert Hall, with its distinctive circular structure atop the main performance venue, overlooks the Motala River.

Overlooking the Motala River in the heart of this former textile center is a new concert hall and meeting facility. It has been fashioned from two of the mills that made the city prosperous, and it anchors a wide-ranging preservation effort known as the "Industrial Landscape."

The overall restoration, which has been taking shape over time, already constitutes a dramatic presence in mid-Norrköping. At least thirty mills, most dating from the nineteenth century, line the Motala. They are handsome brick buildings (some red, others a distinctive yellow), and a number of them already have new uses, while others await rediscovery. When completely restored, this group of structures will be one of the world's most compelling monuments to the Industrial Revolution.

The textile tradition here dates back to the seventeenth century, when Louis de Geer established the first factory beside the river. Textile production was built on an already well-established tradition of crafts in the city, and by the eighteenth century Norrköping had developed into Sweden's third largest trading center. There were once hundreds of trades, but textiles became the dominant industry.

This evolution parallels industrial development in other such centers as Manchester, UK, and, later, Lowell, Massachusetts (see p. 191). Small wool, silk and linen factories were merged into larger units as machinery came into use. Cotton mills began to produce large quantities. Steam engines replaced water power.

The beginning of the end for Norrköping's textile trade came at the turn of the century, when overseas competition began to have an effect on the market. The two world wars kept the factories operating, but by the 1950s they began closing down. The last textile mill closed in 1992.

While the Louis de Geer Hall is the cornerstone of the Industrial Landscape project, there are other major conversions in progress. The Norrköping City Museum is housed in a former mill complex, and the Museum of Work occupies a seven-story mill building on the river. Walkways already in place along the river allow closeup views of the waterfalls, and extensions are being built, all of which feature excellent detailing.

New industries are also moving into the old mills. The Norrköping Informatics Center occupies one mill, which is populated with computer and technology firms. Other uses include space for businesses based on the old crafts tradition. A fitness studio makes use of one of the large halls.

The cylindrical de Geer concert hall, occupying one of the mill buildings, seats 1,300. Its silver domed roof is the most visible part of the conversion. There is a meeting room with a capacity for 200 and a gallery with seating for 800. There are also eight conference rooms.

The front of the Louis de Geer Hall, a welcoming modern addition to a long mill building is part of a formal entrance square to the industrial district. The square is enclosed by a restored yellow brick building that houses offices. A tributary of the river has been restored and now flows under an entrance walkway and joins the main branch of the Motala beside the concert hall. A cafe is located on a grass park beside the river.

Holmentornet, the Holmen Tower built in 1750,

marks the symbolic entryway to a cluster of mills,

most from the 19th century, now gradually

being restored.

LEFT: **Landscaped Kvanholmensplan square, with the concert hall behind, features granite riverside seating.**

BELOW: **The Museum of Work overlooks the dramatic falls of the Motala River.**

The Museum of Work, situated in a textile facility formerly known as "The Rock," opened in 1991. Its 1995 program included material on the human rights movement and on child labor, as well as an exhibit of photos by Ulla Lemberg entitled "Women of the World." There is a museum shop and a cafe with river views on an upper floor. The museum is supported by trade unions.

The City Museum, opened in 1981, features displays from the crafts era, as well as a model of a working loom and documentary information on the lives of textile workers. It is housed in two old craft and industrial houses and two small factory buildings. There is a cafe with tables placed beside the river in a tree-covered setting.

Louis de Geer Hall, with its handsome plaza and waterside arrangement, symbolizes the resilience of this textile-based city. Much as the factories replaced the crafts workers of an earlier time, today a variety of new uses—industrial, technological, educational and public—are reinvigorating the stunning old mill buildings. The falls in the middle of the complex are striking, and so is the ambitious restoration taking place here.

ABOVE: **The falls are a dramatic setting for a mill building from the area's industrial heyday.**

LEFT: **The entrance to the Louis de Geer Concert and Congress (conference) Hall, which was named after the first major industrialist of Norrköping.**

RIGHT: **A pedestrian bridge leads to the entrance of the Museum of Work, which is housed in a seven-story industrial building known as "The Iron."**

129

PUERTO MADERO

Buenos Aires,
ARGENTINA

project name	Puerto Madero
water body	Rio de la Plata
size	420 acres (site); 2 million square meters (building)
cost	$1.8 billion
completion date	1993
sponsor	Corporación Antiguo Puerto Madero S.A.
designer	Juan Carlos Lopez y Asociados S.A.; Patricia Arturi Arquitecta; Samuel Szusterman y Asociados
contact person	Gonzalo W.P. Bunge
	Corporación Antiguo Puerto Madero
	Esmerelda 288, 4th piso
	Buenos Aires 1035
	Argentina
	Tel. 54 1 313 0379 Fax 54 1 313 9698

The sixteen brick warehouses that constitute the primary historic asset of the Puerto Madero project in downtown Buenos Aires are among the most handsome port structures anywhere. The site lies at the foot of the central business district, to which it is read-ily accessible, and faces a large green park that lies along the Rio de la Plata.

The warehouses were built in the 1880s by port engineer Eduardo Madero and lined up along enclosed basins that were based on English models.

The site plan shows the four rectangular docks of Puerto Madero, center, with the Buenos Aires central business district at left.

The entire project was quickly outmoded. Ships became too large to maneuver into the basins and only thirty years after its inception the area was supplanted by Puerto Nuevo (New Port).

Planned redevelopment of this area, extraordinarily enough, dates back to 1925. It is said that every national administration since then has developed its own scheme: the national palace is nearby and the president of Argentina has always had a major say in the affairs of the city.

In 1989, Corporación Antiguo Puerto Madero, an independent development corporation formed equally by the city and national government, each of whom appoints six directors, came into being. The 420 acres that constitute Puerto Madero, including the 16 warehouses, were turned over to the Corporación for development.

An architectural competition was held, and three winning teams were selected in February 1992. Three architects from each team then set about perfecting a final plan for the restoration and development of the area. Envisioned are a fairground, exhibition center and hotel, a recreation and cultural area, historic vessels (one is already in place) and a large central green park across from the docks and warehouses. A mix of uses in the warehouses—office space, condominiums and restaurants—is a goal of the plan.

The strategy of Corporación Antiguo Puerto Madero is simple: with the proceeds from sale of the warehouses it acquires operating funds (there are no state or city subsidies) and the money with which to undertake public improvements.

With the initial sale and development, which has succeeded in bringing offices, cafes and residents

to the area, the Corporación undertook the first improvements, which totaled about $20 million. These included an investment in the supply of electricity and natural gas, as well as water and sewer networks, telephone and satellite facilities.

Public amenities include street improvements and the construction of a continuous pedestrian walkway along the docks. Already in place beside the first restored warehouses, and punctuated with leftover cranes, this wide, landscaped walk is a popular destination. Built on an old rail line that served the docks, it is three thousand meters long and is lined with well-designed street furniture. Old paving stones and railroad ties have been incorporated into the scheme.

The individual warehouses, having different sponsors and architects, exhibit interesting variations of restoration techniques. Early on the Corporación took a crucial step in insuring the preservation of the buildings by having the warehouses, wharves and docks declared an "Area of Patrimonial Protection."

Each warehouse is four stories high and is divided into pavilions. Each pavilion has a freight lift and staircase, with galleries and platforms on the dock side where winches hauled up goods. The original windows were made of iron bars and the gateways for

goods were iron and wood. The interiors of the structures were dilapidated, but much of the goods-handling gear remained behind.

In autumn 1992, four additional warehouses were sold and four more were awarded to the Argentine Catholic University, which will develop the buildings into a campus.

Already there are 1,500 people working in Puerto Madero and four hundred residents. The cafes along the docks are popular installations in a city that is not without significant restaurant attractions. Businesses are aided by the fact that at present small ships still call here at the old port. A small maritime museum ship is docked in one of the basins.

A cloud on the horizon for Puerto Madero is an expressway project that would run overhead. In a plan that dates back to the 1970s, before Puerto Madero was launched, the expressway proposal had enough momentum to have the superstructure, which is now aimed directly at the first warehouse of Dock One, built, but Corporación officials are hopeful of being able to defeat the project. If they are successful, Puerto Madero will take a place with the great waterfront redevelopments of the world.

Each warehouse was restored by a different architect under general design guidelines, resulting in a variety of treatments.

131

A sense of the scale of Puerto Madero is suggested by the 3,000-meter-long promenade. This dock is one of four; there are three more at rear.

THE ROCKS

Sydney,
New South Wales, *AUSTRALIA*

project name	The Rocks
water body	Sydney Cove
size	52 acres
cost	Aus. $2.2 billion
completion date	1970–
sponsor	Sydney Cove Redevelopment Authority
designers	Tropman and Tropman Architects, Sydney
contact person	Geoffrey Bailey
	Sydney Cove Authority
	80 George Street
	Sydney NSW 2000
	Australia
	Tel. 61 2 255 1700
	Fax 61 2 251 1689

**The waterfront precinct of The Rocks features
restored warehouses dating from 1838, left,
and a new hotel, right.**

The story of The Rocks, site of the first European settlement in Australia, is that of a heartening rescue that reflects a sea change in the general attitude toward historic preservation that occurred in many parts of the world in the 1970s.

The idea in the beginning was to extend the Sydney central business district into the adjoining Rocks area by constructing new office towers. The first planning scheme of the Sydney Cove Authority, the government-sponsored redevelopment agency established in 1970, called for office space for thirty thousand people. That same year, the Rocks Residents Action Group was formed, and effectively the battle was begun.

The Rocks, like many an older waterfront district, had its share of derelict buildings, crime and outmoded infrastructure. It was, in fact, Sydney's most unsavory district, and street gangs terrorized the neighborhood. Many buildings had been lost earlier in the century in an effort to eradicate bubonic plague,

and construction of the harbor bridge in the 1920s also demolished part of the area.

However, despite outward appearances of a slum, the Rocks was a viable postwar neighborhood. Its fight to preserve what was left typifies the spark that led to the worldwide historic preservation movement in the 1970s.

With the backing of the Builders Labourers Federation, the Rocks citizens succeeded in placing what were termed "Green Bans" on the area, effectively barring all demolition, construction or restoration. This tactic led, by 1975, to a review of the authority's planning approach, and to the decision that in the future greater emphasis would be placed on "cultural, social and historic values and less on economic returns." The Rocks was saved.

Today, it is a source of considerable pride, not only to the Sydney Cove Authority but to all of Sydney, that this historic place—where in 1788 Captain Arthur Phillips landed and established the

RIGHT: **The tower of the Australian Steamship Navigation Co. building, 1885, features Flemish gables.**

BELOW LEFT: **A weekend street market is a popular event. The roofline of the Sydney Opera House is visible at rear.**

ABOVE: **The new Park Hyatt Hotel, beneath Sydney Harbour Bridge, was designed to fit into the historic Rocks area.**

RIGHT: **The welcoming rear façades of shops along George Street.**

British Empire's most distant outpost, a penal colony —has been preserved. New construction is allowed to be undertaken but under strict guidelines that require conformity to the existing buildings in scale, material and color. A triumph in this realm is the design of the Park Hyatt Hotel, which has been kept to three stories, is made of brick that blends with nearby historic warehouses and has a generous public walkway along its bay frontage.

Today, twenty-five years after the start of the preservation effort, the emphasis at the Rocks is on restored buildings being used to house an interesting array of shops and pubs, on inviting walkways and on educational displays that relate the local history.

The Rocks, right, was saved from the encroachment of the central business district, which rises up at rear. Ferry docks at Circular Quay, center.

The Rocks would be a pleasant precinct in any city, combining narrow streets, interesting architecture, history and culture with stylish restaurants and pubs close to harbor walkways with spectacular views of the Sydney Harbour Bridge overhead, and everything a short walk from downtown and Sydney's efficient ferry system. Also nearby, within easy reach by car or on foot, are some of the city's other highlights: the Opera House (see pp. 112–3), the Botanic Garden and the art museum. In the other direction are the attractions of Darling Harbour (see pp. 40–3).

The Rocks is now a prime visitor site. Its fifty or so acres, nestled between the cove and the highway approaches to the harbor bridge, are a testimony to the effort of the citizens who took to the streets in 1973 to protest against the planned unsympathetic development. What they fought to preserve is today a center of history and entertainment, a viable neighborhood and an economic success.

CHAPTER 5

The Recreational
Waterfront

The appeal of spending leisure time on the water is a common theme in recent urban waterfront developments around the globe. Wherever fences are cut open or private waterfront land is traversed, this desire is made physically apparent. Whether for fishing, swimming or quiet contemplation, and in spite of barriers, intrepid urban dwellers will gravitate toward whatever water body they live near.

Though often obscured by the attention given to more architecturally exciting commercial and cultural projects, in sheer acreage and in community impact, the newly created public spaces—major parks, walkways and trail systems, marinas and neighborhood play areas—constitute the biggest change along today's urban waterfront.

Dramatically different in their geography and culture, the Parc de la Villette in Paris, the Swansea Maritime Quarter, the Kuching Waterfront in Malaysia and Sumidagawa River Walkway in Tokyo all associate relaxation and enjoyment with being on the water.

Typical of these initiatives is the Sumidagawa River Walkway in central Tokyo. In just five years an inaccessible and deteriorated riverfront has been transformed by the addition of an extensive walkway system and beautiful landscaping, with shade pavilions, distinctive paving and lighted fountains adding to the pleasant atmosphere. The project is a remarkable achievement in a country that until recently had not demonstrated much concern for public use of its waterfronts. The walkway, with its numerous connections to nearby streets and to the city's subway system, represents the opening up of the riverfront to the residents of Tokyo.

In a grandiose gesture costing $340 million, the city of Düsseldorf, Germany, recaptured the Rhine riverfront for public use in 1994 by putting a highway underground. A tunnel two kilometers long replaced a surface roadway that handled fifty thousand cars a day and had effectively sealed off access to the river from the nearby city. Residents can now frequent a large new waterfront park (see p. 208).

In Hong Kong, where space is at a premium, recent efforts have added a significant number of new waterfront parks, walkways and promenades that are part of new town developments and other projects (see pp. 197–8). Extensive pieces of a major walkway system have been put in place along the Thames in London (see pp. 212–3). In Auckland, New Zealand, people can walk or bike for miles along the harborfront where an elaborate pedestrian overpass has been installed to link a downtown neighborhood with the shoreline. In Singapore along East Coast Park, a massive park and pathway has been created on landfill (see p. 201). These are some examples of the way cities around the world are responding to the popularity of waterfront recreation.

It is a safe predication that the predominate new use for urban waterfront land in coming decades will be for recreational and related cultural spaces that will then be served by restaurants and other commercial facilities that enhance the experience of being on the waterfront.

We have a priceless beauty spot in our river and could easily make it so that homes and even business places would be remodeled to face the river instead of having their back doors to it. The plan drawn up proposed to build stairways down to the riverbank … and to place benches there for the use of the public.

Robert H. H. Hugman
on the Paseo del Rio, San Antonio, 1935

OPPOSITE: **The Tees Barrage has helped to clean up the polluted River Tees in England, sparking regeneration along 19 miles of riverfront (see p. 217).**

See these projects in the Gazetteer:

SWANSEA MARITIME QUARTER

Swansea,
Wales, UK

project name	Swansea Maritime Quarter
water body	River Tawe, Swansea Bay and South Dock
size	95 acres
cost	£117 million
completion date	1975–
sponsor	City of Swansea
designers	6 different practices
contact person	David Wilson
	City of Swansea
	West Glamorgan SA1
	Wales, UK
	Tel. 44 1792 301 301
	Fax 44 1792 302 719

The site of the South Dock basin of Swansea was once the center of the city's social and political life, marked by Georgian houses and gardens and long promenades by the sea. The needs of the copper trade around which the economy was built led in the 1850s to construction, despite citizens' protests, of South Dock. Until its opening in 1859, vessels using the Swansea harbor were subject to the tidal fluctuations on the River Tawe.

South Dock was a large, self-contained basin with a controlled water level, and ship traffic in Swansea doubled in ten years as a result of its construction. Surrounding the basin were elevated railways, warehouses, offices and coal hoists. With the building of the basin Swansea's waterfront changed from being a seaside resort area to an industrial precinct. Chapels, missions, hotels and pubs moved in as the waterfront began to thrive.

Then economics again dictated a change for the dock area. Local metal industries could not compete globally, and by 1969 the South Dock was closed down and purchased by the city council. After resisting efforts to fill in the basin, the council set about turning its derelict property into an asset and began rebuilding its infrastructure in 1975.

Swansea's Maritime Quarter today represents a complete return to its origins. If it is not the center of the city's cultural life, it is nonetheless a successfully reconstituted neighborhood blending new apartments with a range of visitor accommodations, a historic district and a major recreational boat harbor. The seaside promenade has returned and is distinguished by numerous pieces of public art.

The curved, two-level promenade runs between a wide beach on Swansea Bay and residential clusters, right.

ABOVE: **The Astronomical Society facility houses a 360 mm reflecting telescope, viewing galleries and exhibition space at the top of the structure at right.**

LEFT: **Anchoring the eastern end of the beachfront promenade is the Swansea Astronomical Society's twin structures, including the Tower of the Ecliptic.**

139

On the north side of South Dock is an historic district with fifteen buildings that are gradually being converted for a range of new uses, including residences and cultural attractions. Among the latter is a museum focusing on the life and work of Swansea native Dylan Thomas, a Dylan Thomas theater, formerly a garage, and a seamen's chapel that has been converted into an art gallery.

While many buildings around the dock were demolished, the council saved and converted the large, centrally located 1900 Coastal Lines Warehouse for use as an industrial and maritime museum. A repository for many marine artifacts, it also has a transportation component. Exhibits range from parts of a woolen mill to historic vessels docked outside. Another preserved building is the Pumphouse, also built in 1900, a restaurant/pub. Its

tower housed the machinery that operated the swing bridge and locks.

South Dock itself was rehabilitated in 1982 and is now a boat basin with a capacity for four hundred vessels. New clusters of apartments have been built around it, both permanent and holiday residences. A range of styles and sizes ensures a mixed population. While some of the apartments are of standard, even somewhat suburban design, others are of a distinctive architectural quality. The area is marked by public art and large public squares that demonstrate the attention that has been paid to details and enhancement of the public space. Craft pieces include carved plaques, imaginative wind vanes, and sculptures representing both mythological and maritime themes.

One of the most unusual installations is that of the Swansea Astronomical Society, whose tower on the

seaside promenade houses telescopes. The lighthouse is a combined painted-steel and glass structure that sits atop a stone tower. At the eastern end of the promenade is a mermaid carved from a block of sandstone.

Along the river frontage is a mixture of new and old construction, including the Swansea Angling Center, Olde Pilot House Cafe and Sea Cadet Corps headquarters. A long walkway stretches out over the harbor entrance jetty.

New high-speed gates allow boats into the River Tawe and out to the sea. With the addition of the barrage, the river has become a major moorage area for recreational boats, which means that the name of "Maritime Quarter" given to this conversion is not just a marketing slogan.

SUMIDAGAWA RIVER WALKWAY

Tokyo,
JAPAN

project name	Sumidagawa River Walkway
water body	Sumidagawa River
size	28.4 kilometers
cost	$822 million
completion date	1990–
sponsor	River Division, Bureau of Construction
	Tokyo Metropolitan Government
contact person	Yasuo Takahashi
	River Division, Bureau of Construction
	Tokyo Metropolitan Government
	22 Floor, 2nd Tower
	2-8-1 Nishinjuku, 2-chome
	Shinjuku-ku, 163-01 Tokyo
	Japan
	Tel. 81 3 5320 5413 Fax 81 3 5388 1533

Planned to run seventeen miles along both sides of the Sumidagawa River when completed in the year 2000, the Sumidagawa walkway represents a change in Tokyo's civic planning philosophy.

When the banks of the river were stabilized for flood protection years ago, little thought was given to either aesthetics or public enjoyment. As recently as 1990, the downtown section of the Sumidagawa was lined with unappealing concrete that was only occasionally punctuated by an office building's landscaped garden.

There are now large segments of a beautifully detailed walkway in place. Where once there were blank walls there are now elaborate plantings, gazebos, tiles with historic wood-block prints of the river and a graceful railing featuring fish, birds and other artistic details. With these improvements the planners have effectively provided the congested city with a significant amount of accessible open space.

The Tokyo Metropolitan Government is undertaking the project in sections and improving along the way: the paving and other details in the most recent effort are more carefully done than in the first portions. A notable feature of the walkway is the variety of pavement patterns that are used—all artfully designed and incorporating different materials. The new walkway runs beside both apartments and offices in central Tokyo, and even passes through the famous Ginza district.

The walkway course from the Asakusa subway station toward the harbor features eleven bridges, each of which are of a different design. The oldest dates from 1926, and some are modeled on examples from such places as Chicago and Cologne.

A formally landscaped river terrace enhances the walkways along the left bank of the Sumidagawa River in downtown Tokyo.

RIGHT: **Pergolas with shaded seating are pleasant spots from which to enjoy the view.**

BELOW: **Sculptures, decorative railings and varied paving distinguish the Sumidagawa riverwalk.**

The walkway is below grade level in some places and is screened from the adjoining road by flood walls in others. It is easily accessed by stairs descending from the bridges, which means pedestrians are below the noise and traffic. Although both sides of the river are heavily built up and an expressway crosses it from west to east and runs upriver, the atmosphere on the walkway is relatively quiet and serene. Landscaping alongside the concrete walls also enhances the walk, while pergolas and other features provide shaded rest areas. There is seating throughout, as well as steps beside the flood walls where the walkway space is wide, and green banks slope gently down toward the river's edge.

At the northern end of the walkway, near the Asakusa subway, is an enormous underground bicy-cle storage facility. Bicycles are racked and locked in a brightly lit space that is used by commuters and strollers alike.

Now a major tourist attraction, this section of the Sumidagawa is cruised by tour boats that can hold as many as 550 passengers. The river has been an important thoroughfare for commerce since the Edo period and, despite flooding incidents, continues to loom large in the history of Tokyo.

PARC DE LA VILLETTE/CITY OF SCIENCE AND INDUSTRY

Paris,
FRANCE

project name	Parc de la Villette/Cité des Sciences et de l'Industrie
water body	St. Denis Canal and l'Ourcq Canal
size	136 acres
cost	$256.5 million (museum)
completion date	1979–; 1986 (museum)
sponsor	Etablissement Public du Parc de la Villette
designers	Prof. Bernard Tschumi (master plan)
	Adrien Fainsilber (City of Science and Industry)
contact person	Julia Fainsilber
	Adrien Fainsilber, Architecte
	7 rue Salvador Allende
	Nanterre 92000
	France
	Tel. 33 47 21 64 38 Fax 33 47 21 58 08

**The City of Science and Industry contains
1,776,060 square feet of space. The steel globe
of the Geode, which houses a cinema, is at right.**

Baron Haussmann, the Paris master planner, deposited the municipal slaughterhouses on the eastern side of the city in 1862. They, along with coal storage facilities and a cattle market, remained in the area, which became increasingly unfashionable, until 1974. When those were abandoned, the district became even more rundown. The Canal de l'Ourcq splits this 136-acre site while Canal St. Denis forms the western edge. Metro stations are located at the northern and southern boundaries.

The transformation of the area began in 1984. Over the next decade, a multifaceted urban park was built in the place of the one-time industrial/transportation hub. Parc de la Villette's signature building, la Cité des Sciences et de l'Industrie (the City of Science and Industry), is a giant slaughterhouse, the conversion of which began in 1950 but was interrupted before completion.

The building was excavated down to the base of the large concrete pillars that formed its foundation in order to let in large amounts of natural light. Landscaped terraces with waterfalls descend to the pool surrounding the museum. There are three large greenhouses on the south façade facing the Geode, a steel globe that houses a film theater, as well as green open space along the canal.

The structure contains 1.7 million square feet of space. In addition to fascinating permanent displays, there is an auditorium with a seating capacity of one thousand, a library, children's discovery area, cinema, restaurant and shops. Architect Adrien Fainsilber was chosen to design the facility, along with Sylvain Mersier, in a competition that was held in 1980. The

The distinctive form of the Geode marks the south

façade of the City of Science and Industry on the

Canal de l'Ourcq.

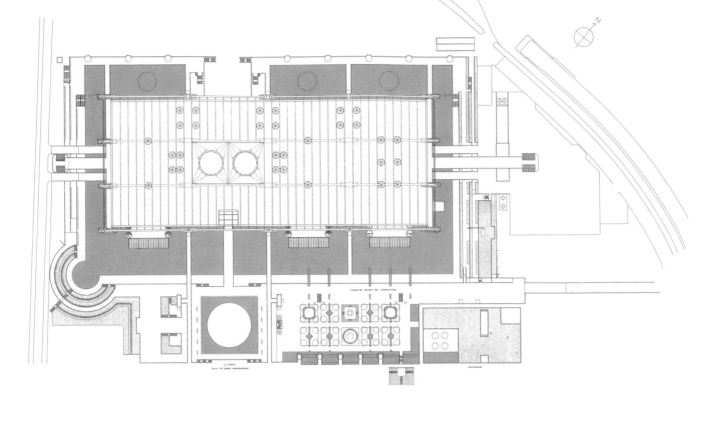

scale: 1:1500 meters

conversion, which cost $261 million, was completed in 1986. The park now attracts five million visitors each year.

The other main feature, the Grande Halle, was built in 1867 as the first slaughterhouse. Its cast-iron columns now support glass walls. It has been converted to serve today as a multipurpose venue that hosts concerts and exhibitions, with a seating capacity of fifteen thousand.

Along the canals are the park's hallmarks, bright red follies that are arrayed throughout in a grid pattern. They number twenty-four and range in use from metal sculptures to a first-aid station.

Between the science and industry museum and exhibition hall are a variety of other attractions and large greenswards. An information center is housed in the former Veterinarians Hall, and directly in front of the science and industry museum the Geode's silver surface reflects the surrounding pool and the sky.

A bicycle path runs for six miles alongside the Canal de l'Ourcq, beginning at the Rond-Point des Canaux, where four canals intersect. There is also a cruise-boat dock. A newer addition at the southern end of the park is the Cité de la Musique, a complex devoted to music and dance. It contains a concert hall and a museum, as well as a small theater, a contemporary music center and the Paris national conservatory. Le Zenith, a rock music hall, is located in another section.

Parc de la Villette is thus a classic urban waterfront conversion that has completely remade and revitalized an abandoned canal-side location in the heart of Paris.

ABOVE: **The plan of the City of Science and Industry shows the moat surrounding the structure.**

BELOW: **Cross-sections show the details of the City**

of Science and Industry building in relation

to the Geode.

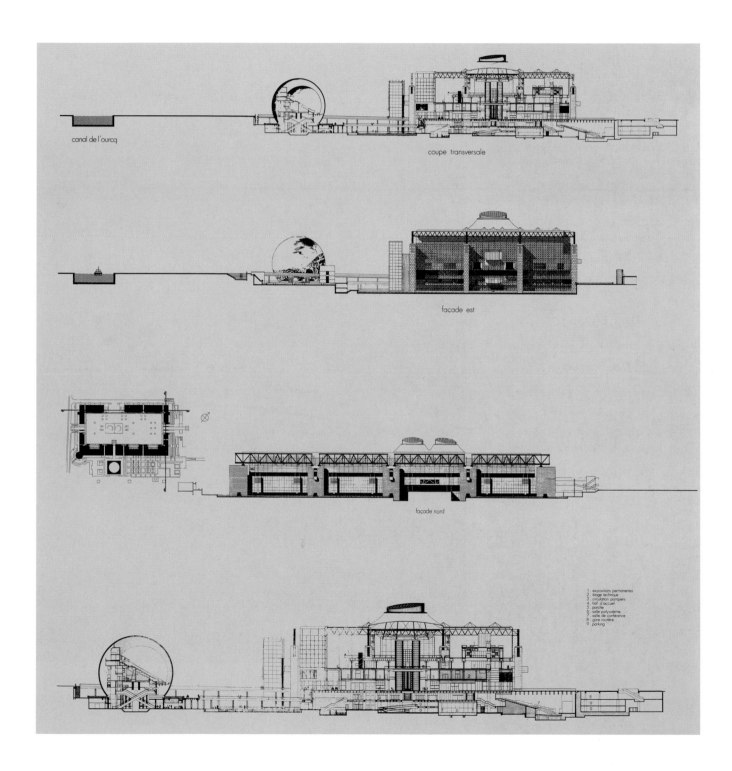

canal de l'ourcq

coupe transversale

façade est

façade nord

A map diagram at the park entrance illustrates the attractions contained in the 136 acres of former industrial land on the east side of Paris.

ABOVE: **A moat surrounding the City of Science and Industry reflects the glass, steel and concrete structure, which was originally a slaughterhouse.**

RIGHT: **A distinctive red steel "folly," one of 24 such structures that are carefully arrayed throughout the park, sits atop a two-level walkway.**

BELOW: **The curved railing of a canal walkway.**

147

TOP: **Waterfalls punctuate the moat around
the City of Science and Industry.**

RIGHT: **Detail of a canalside walkway called
the Embarcadero.**

BELOW: **The façade of the City of Science and
Industry retains a portion of the original concrete
construction.**

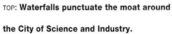

KUCHING WATERFRONT DEVELOPMENT

Kuching,
Sarawak, *MALAYSIA*

project name	Kuching Waterfront Redevelopment
water body	Sarawak River
size	I kilometer
completion date	1993
sponsor	State Economic Development Corporation
designers	Conybeare Morrison and Partners
contact person	William Morrison
	Conybeare Morrison and Partners
	346 Kent Street
	Sydney, NSW 1035
	Australia
	Tel. 61 2 299 5711
	Fax 61 2 262 4785

The redevelopment of the old Kuching waterfront near the heart of the city is as bold and dramatic as will be found anywhere. By its opening in September 1993, an area formerly characterized by deterioration, abandonment and squalid living conditions had been transformed into a beautiful new promenade and public space.

As in many cases, the central port facilities in Kuching, a major trading and administrative center, had relocated over the years, and the river walls of

OPPOSITE: **A promenade, park, belvederes, rotunda, tea terraces and amphitheater are among the features of the Kuching Waterfront Development.**

BELOW: **The master plan was prepared by Conybeare Morrison and Partners of Sydney, Australia.**

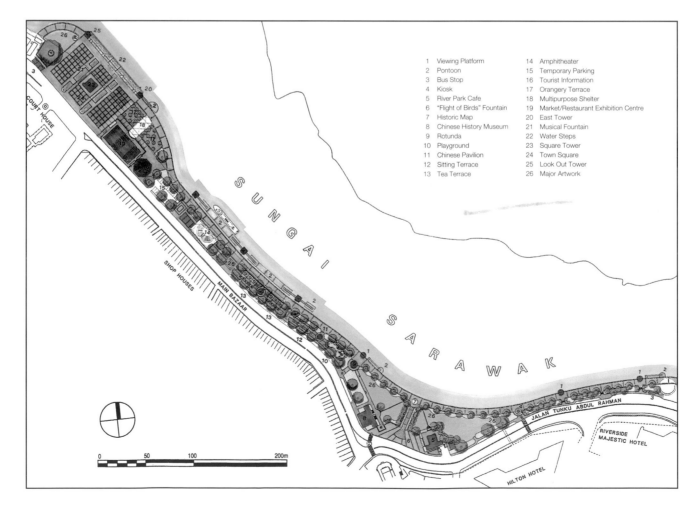

1	Viewing Platform	14	Amphitheater
2	Pontoon	15	Temporary Parking
3	Bus Stop	16	Tourist Information
4	Kiosk	17	Orangery Terrace
5	River Park Cafe	18	Multipurpose Shelter
6	"Flight of Birds" Fountain	19	Market/Restaurant Exhibition Centre
7	Historic Map	20	East Tower
8	Chinese History Museum	21	Musical Fountain
9	Rotunda	22	Water Steps
10	Playground	23	Square Tower
11	Chinese Pavilion	24	Town Square
12	Sitting Terrace	25	Look Out Tower
13	Tea Terrace	26	Major Artwork

149

LEFT: **Looking west along the Sarawak River. The Town Square is marked by a five-story observation tower, top center.**

ABOVE RIGHT: **Shaded pavilions are located throughout the park and on viewing platforms that extend over the river.**

the central waterfront deteriorated. Squatter camps grew up, wharves and warehouses were abandoned and the river's edge was degraded and used for rubbish disposal.

The new project stretches almost one kilometer in length and ties the Sarawak River to the center of Kuching. The main features include a new river wall; a wide, shaded promenade; a handsomely landscaped waterfront park; cantilevered belvederes over the river, and restored historic buildings.

Exceptional design details were fashioned by a partnership of an Australian firm and United Consultants of Kuching, working for the State Economic Development Corp. The paving, artworks, decorations and promenade wall all draw on the rich cultural heritage of the island of Borneo—its mix of ethnic populations and its colonial history.

Thirteen different mosaic patterns are used in the paving, and designs on the river-wall balustrade are based on a traditional Chinese motif. Pavilion roofs

ABOVE: **The observation tower at the new Town
Square is a symbol of the rejuvenated waterfront
along the Sarawak River.**

LEFT: **The "Flight of Birds" fountain and pools
are illuminated at night.**

BELOW: **The observation tower and kiosks are
silhouetted against a Malaysian sunset.**

151

likewise are influenced by colorful, traditional designs.
Planting is lush, and attractive street furniture and
light fixtures and an imaginative nighttime illumination
scheme have been used.

The centerpiece of the Kuching Waterfront Development Project is a new Town Square waterfront park
containing a nineteenth-century square tower flanked
by pools and fountains. This previously neglected city
symbol now houses a history and audio-visual center.
The square has become a favorite gathering spot for
visitors and the local population alike.

This public project has brought about a revitalization of the nearby commercial area. By re-establish-
ing vistas and visible connections to the city center, it
has also physically and symbolically reunited Kuching
with its historic riverfront.

CHAPTER 6

The Residential
Waterfront

Occupying anything from the humblest of stilt huts or makeshift houseboats to the grandest châteaux and skyscrapers, people throughout history have been living along the water for reasons both practical and poetic. Waterside living is so attractive that today developers create artificial lakes and ponds to build housing around. An axiom in the real-estate trade is that the same residence on a water body will command a higher price than its landlocked counterpart. Despite the danger of hurricanes and floods, people continue to build and rebuild in coastal and river locations. The growing demand for private residences on the water is a significant part of the phenomenon of "the new waterfront."

The home is a private place, but the water rivers, lakes, coasts and canals are inherently public resources. This opposition creates tension between the two groups when the public's desire to be near the water clashes with the individual property owner's desire for privacy and security.

When a project is thoughtfully planned and executed, as are the residential schemes described here, private needs are incorporated with ample public access. In these cases the space along the water's edge is welcoming to visitors as well as to the immediate residential population. That they are "welcoming" means that walkways and facilities are not just present, but that they are visible, attractive and accessible, and that non-residents feel comfortable using them.

An unfortunate tendency among waterfront residential projects, particularly those at the high end economically, is the attempt to seal themselves off from the public. They use the obvious physical barriers, such as fences and guardhouses, or they create a psychological sense that the space beside the water "belongs" to the residents and that outsiders are not wanted.

A welcome balance between private and public interests is achieved when new waterfront housing precincts contain social or subsidized housing. Successful examples include the Entrepot West Amsterdam project, built in a city with a strong tradition of social housing; and Columbia Point in Boston, where, as in most US cities, public housing is generally located in a ghetto district (see p. 188). The Columbia Point Housing Project took one such failed housing area and converted it into an economically and racially mixed, well-designed neighborhood that enjoys splendid views of Boston harbor. Another scheme that incorporates subsidized units is the Tegel Harbor Project in Berlin. Likewise, the city-sponsored Ruoholahti development in Helsinki has a considerable amount of subsidized housing.

Styles in housing inevitably vary according to culture. Perhaps the most dramatic developments illustrated in this book are the new towns of Hong Kong (see p. 198). In South Horizons New Town, for instance, the new residential community consists of a cluster of high-rise towers. For many, this approach would seem claustrophobic. For landlocked areas of Hong Kong, a city that has for years been working to replace old, substandard dwellings for its burgeoning population, the high-rise concentration makes sense —indeed, so limited is the land and rugged the terrain, it may be the only option. Dispersed development here might easily have destroyed precious open space.

Whether they are in a high-rise on the harbor in Hong Kong, an apartment in Manhattan overlooking the Hudson River, or a warehouse loft in London on the Thames, people will continue to settle along the water. As a consequence, the tension between private and public interests with respect to that most public of resources will continue and, most likely, increase as communities seek to redevelop their waterfront.

It was my thirtieth year to heaven
*   Woke to my hearing from harbour and*
neighbor wood
*   And the mussel pooled and the heron*
*   Priested shore*
*   The morning beckon*
*   With water praying and call of the seagull*
and rook
*   And the knock of sailing boats on the*
net webbed wall

Dylan Thomas, "Poem in October," 1944

OPPOSITE: **Flagship Wharf, part of new housing complex at the former Boston Navy Yard in Charlestown.**

153

See these projects in the Gazetteer:

Columbia Point Housing Project, Boston, USA
South Horizons, Hong Kong
Rokko Island, Kobe, Japan
Mazzorbo Housing Project, Venice, Italy

ENTREPOT WEST

Amsterdam,
THE NETHERLANDS

project name	Entrepot West, Amsterdam
water body	Entrepot Harbor
size	524 dwelling units
cost	DFl. 65 million
completion date	1993
sponsor	Woonstichting de Doelen Amsterdam
designers	Atelier PRO
contact person	Leon Thier/Hans van Beek
	Atelier PRO
	Kerkhofcaan 11A
	The Hague 2585 JB
	The Netherlands
	Tel. 31 7 035 06900 Fax 31 7 035 14971

154

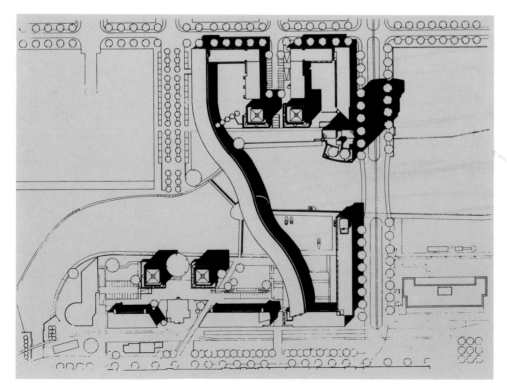

Site plan of Entrepot West, showing the curved apartment building over the water that is the project's signature.

When the eastern docks of Amsterdam relocated to accommodate larger vessels, a major tract of land became available for development. The main drawback was its relative isolation from central Amsterdam and the prospect of a new roadway that would further separate the two areas. To enable the city to reuse the docks for a housing precinct, the road was put in a tunnel below ground, and plans were made to extend public transport to the area.

Amsterdam city planners meanwhile developed a program to create an entirely new residential neighborhood among the old docks that would preserve the warehouse structures, and they began issuing commissions for work on individual piers. The entire project, the Oostelijk Havengebied redevelopment, is due for completion around the year 2000.

One of the major components of this project was completed in 1993 in an existing neighborhood on the Entrepot harbor. Instead of a giant block, as suggested by the original city scheme, Atelier PRO of The Hague prepared a plan that has as its centerpiece a curved, six-story structure that bridges the main water body in the tract and has a bottom level that is open to waterfront views. The building has become an Amsterdam landmark and a minor tourist attraction.[1] Architect Hans van Beek notes that the very first proposals for the area called for draining the water; however, today the former harbor is the main attraction.

The project's 524 housing units are distributed in a variety of buildings of differing styles. Heights generally range from four to eight stories, with a fourteen-story tower as anchor on the northern side. The main

BELOW: **Care was taken to retain a monumental tree on the site, now rising up between two apartment buildings.**

BOTTOM: **A former cocoa warehouse, center, was converted into a library/resource center. Warehouses at left will become apartments.**

155

parking area is sensibly placed underground beneath a courtyard, making Entrepot West a pedestrian district. Towers with upscale apartments have their own parking. Given the careful design and landscaping, it is worth noting that seventy-seven percent of the housing has subsidized rent.

An old customs office of brick construction, flanked by two apartment buildings, has been preserved and is now used for a kindergarten. Care has also been taken to retain a monumental tree in the area. The old customs wall in the harbor has been turned into a promenade which leads to a waterfront restaurant located in the middle of the project.

159

PREVIOUS PAGES: **The curved, six-story apartment building at the center of the project is known locally as "the Slinger."**

FAR LEFT: **The eastern façade. The undulating building is set on pillars over the water; a restaurant is on the first level.**

ABOVE: **Balconies and window treatments form a bold geometric pattern. Over three-quarters of the 524 apartments have subsidized rents.**

LEFT: **A graceful solution to the building code requirement for external fire escapes.**

TEGEL HARBOR

Berlin,
GERMANY

project name	Tegel Harbor Redevelopment
water body	Tegel Sea
size	40 acres
completion date	1987
sponsor	Senator für Stadtentwicklung und Umweltschutz
designers	Moore Ruble Yudell; various (housing)
contact person	Mark Denton
	Moore Ruble Yudell
	993 Pico Blvd.
	Santa Monica, CA 90405
	USA
	Tel. 1 310 450 1400
	Fax 1 310 450 1403

160

Tegel Harbor Housing—public housing of unusual design.

161

The Tegel Harbor complex, consisting of both public and private housing, a library/community center and recreational island, is built on a former industrial precinct.

The harbor atrophied after World War II with the split of East and West Germany; this outpost is located on the western edge of Berlin on the border with the former East Germany, and water traffic in the area had ceased.

A master plan for the forty-acre site, developed in a competition won by Moore Ruble Yudell of Santa Monica, California, is organized around a harbor. In fact, a crucial element of the plan was the extension of the harbor and its expansion toward the traditional center of Tegel. An entry plaza creates a link between Tegel Harbor and the surrounding neighborhood. A nearby subway stop connects Tegel to the heart of

Berlin and puts it within easy reach of residents from throughout the city.

The cultural centerpiece of the project is a striking library, a building that was the personal favorite of the architect, the late Charles Moore. Sitting at one end of the complex, the Humboldt- Bibliothek is a low-lying structure that is at once industrial in feel and natural in its setting, being open to woods on one side. A skylight runs the length of the roof, infusing the interior space with natural light from the south. A wooden ceiling provides a sense of warmth and intimacy. In the children's section of the library a large window faces the harbor. The library also functions as a community center/meeting place and focal point for the Tegel neighborhood.

At the opposite end of the harbor stands a handsome public housing project and play space,

ABOVE: **A pedestrian bridge gives access to the low-lying Humboldt-Bibliothek, a new focal point for the Tegel community in western Berlin.**

BELOW: **A harbor view of the public housing complex; public walkways line both sides of the waterway.**

ABOVE: **The library, at rear, commands a view of the harbor and villas, right.**

RIGHT: **Tegel Harbor Housing has a C-shaped form that surrounds a courtyard.**

BELOW: **The signature arched front window of the library building.**

also designed by Charles Moore. Containing 170 units of subsidized housing, it bears no resemblance to the traditionally drab public housing usually found in the US, but rather curves delightfully around the harbor to end in a courtyard surrounded by five-story structures.

An island in the harbor, linked by pedestrian bridges and accessible by small boats, provides wild, open space. The original plan called for a recreation building, but today it is a thoroughly romantic setting that is separate enough from the surrounding community to have a genuine sense of retreat.

A final element in the scheme is housing designed by an international roster of architects, a bit of a *tour de force* of late-1980s postmodernism. Included are large houses fronting the extended harbor, designed by Stanley Tigerman, Robert A. M. Stern and John Hejduk of the US, and others by the French architect Antoine Grumbach and the Italian Paolo Portoghesi.

Ample public promenades and benches along the shoreline enable people to stroll, sit and enjoy the waterside setting.

LEFT AND RIGHT: **A villa designed by Moore Ruble Yudell, one of a series designed by an international roster of architects.**

163

A sketch of Tegel Harbor Housing, a design of the late Charles Moore of Moore Ruble Yudell of the US.

A view across the lake of the library. At left is a restored mill building that is now a hotel.

FISH MARKET HAMBURG-ALTONA

Hamburg,
GERMANY

project name	Fischmarkt Hamburg-Altona
water body	Elbe River
completion date	1989
designers	Meidhard von Gerkan, Volkwin Marg, von Gerkan, Marg and Partner
contact person	Bernd Pastuschka
	von Gerkan, Marg and Partner
	Elbchaussee 139
	Hamburg 22763
	Germany
	Tel. 49 40 881 510
	Fax 49 40 881 5117

ABOVE: **The new Fischmarkt blends new housing, right, with remaining structures, left.**

RIGHT: **The western façade fronts the plaza. The original fish market is located behind the building.**

This project is the result of a thoroughgoing planning study by the City of Hamburg. Beginning in 1976, as many as twelve alternative approaches were examined for the redevelopment of a one-time flourishing neighborhood that had suffered heavy damage in World War II bombing. Only six of the houses that surrounded the plaza leading to the city's traditional fish market remained.

Dependent on the chosen scheme was the question of what to do with the fish market structure, which had survived the war—how to handle as many as 3,500 vendors who used the market, whether or not to continue traditional Sunday markets in the neighborhood, and, if so, how to organize them effectively.

Work began in 1980, when the flood wall along the Elbe River was built up and a six hundred-meter-long landscaped promenade was created along the river. The market building is outside the wall and still occasionally floods.

Nearby roads were reworked to re-establish the Fischmarkt plaza, which is the focus of the project. It is a lovely wide space, narrow at the top and widening as it descends toward the river, that affords dramatic views of port activity. The site's orientation toward the river and elevated views overcome the physical distance. Rebuilt housing encloses the plaza and gives it a welcoming, protected feel.

Other interventions by the city include the installation of a children's playground in the plaza. A sculpture of a fisherwoman has been carefully restored, and a new pedestrian bridge crosses the roadway that separates the plaza housing and shops from the river's edge.

RIGHT: **A turreted apartment on the corner faces the roadway, the promenade and the River Elbe.**

BELOW: **A view from the top of the plaza toward the River Elbe, with the cranes of the Port of Hamburg clearly visible.**

OPPOSITE: **The project's signature fish weather vane marks the entrance to the Fischmarkt plaza.**

166

The new housing, 173 units total, is arrayed on both sides of the plaza. Each side was designed by different architects following the stipulation that the new units reflect the height, style, colors and rooflines of the existing buildings, and roof tiles were carefully selected to match. The difference between the 1980s apartments and the nineteenth-century buildings is readily detectable, but old and new are so well blended that the entire project appears of a piece. The decision was also taken to build over an entry road on the western side, so that the façade remains unbroken. The apartments, averaging 1,100 square meters, contain a large proportion of social housing.

In 1984 the fish market hall was restored, and for a touch of authenticity bronze figures of fish and other creatures that once decorated the building, but had been melted down during the war for military use, were replicated from documents.

By 1989 the entire project was in place. At the ground level are shops, cafes and restaurants that open onto the ring walkway and give the area a festive air in pleasant weather. The Sunday markets are again filled with shoppers, the plaza is restored to its former vitality and this segment beside the Elbe in Hamburg is alive once again.

R U O H O L A H T I

Helsinki,
FINLAND

project name	Ruoholahti Waterfront
water body	Ruoholahti Bay
size	163 acres
cost	$800 million
completion date	1986–
sponsor	City of Helsinki
designers	Helsinki City Planning and Public Works Depts.
contact person	Annukka Lindroos, Architect
	Helsinki City Planning Dept.
	Kansakoulukatu 3
	Helsinki 00100
	Finland
	Tel. 358 80 169 4211
	Fax 358 80 169 4243

An aerial view of the Ruoholahti project looking toward the West Harbor of Helsinki.

In an industrial and warehousing district near a main cargo port in Finland, a residential and office precinct is being developed that will soon be home to nine thousand people.

The decision to redevelop was made in 1985. Because the territory was city-owned, development came rapidly, beginning two years later with the construction of a metro-line connection. After a planning competition, designs for the office and residential components were approved, and the first residents moved into the area in 1992. Completion is scheduled for the year 2001.

The apartments are, for the most part, five- and six-story blocks, identical to the height and bulk of nearby existing apartment buildings. The look and feel of this brand new addition to downtown Helsinki, immediately to the west of the central business district, is very much in keeping with the surrounding neighborhood.

The office component consists of eight buildings, from six to eight stories tall, that are clustered in two sections. The main office block is adjacent to the metro stop, as is the principal commercial area. There are expected to be 3,500 workers here.

The standard of design and construction is high. Details in the major public spaces, for example, along the canal that was added through the center of the site, are also exceptional.

Several buildings from the previous industrial era are being retained; notable among them is a Cable Factory being developed into an arts and cultural center. It is located at the westernmost part of the site, near a school and offices. A factory and a power

ABOVE: **A pedestrian bridge unites two sections of the project that are split by a canal.**

RIGHT: **A view down the canal toward the city center shows the generous public spaces and canal walkway.**

BELOW: **The project entrance, with a distinctively designed apartment building at right.**

169

station have also been preserved, and the stacks of the latter are now something of a signature for the project.

As with most city-run projects in Scandinavia, there is a strong social commitment. Over half of the apartments are subsidized and will be available either to rent or own. The apartments are of various sizes—with two bedrooms, four bedrooms and some single rooms with kitchenettes—to help bring in a diverse population.

All of the residential blocks contain their own club room and other group facilities, and there are larger club facilities—one featuring sports equipment—that are open to all residents. A public art program has sponsored sculpture and wall murals.

As large an undertaking as Ruoholahti is, it may be only part of a huge new neighborhood that will open up if, as planned, the cargo operations of the adjacent Lansisatama precinct are moved to the east of the city. The entire area is expected to house 22,000 people, all of whom will enjoy access to the waterfront and quality design, if Ruoholahti is followed as an example.

CHAPTER 7

The Working Waterfront
and Transportation

Some of the most powerful and exciting areas of the urban waterfront are associated with the working port and industrial and transportation facilities.

The port, with its giant container cranes and huge vessels gliding in and out of the harbor, is a familiar image. While many port operations are now in remote locations, some functions are still performed in the city center, as in the enormous facilities of Oakland, California, and in Rotterdam and Hamburg.

Heavy industrial equipment, small factories and water-treatment plants, along with such transportation facilities as bridges and cruise-ship terminals all make use of waterfront space and sometimes have a dramatic impact on design.

Still other working waterfront users are small enterprises. Many small marine businesses have been present on the city waterfronts for decades during which no one paid attention to these areas. Such businesses contribute to the character and economic mix of a city, and they are often part of the colorful allure of the waterfront.

Left strictly to economic forces, however, small marine businesses such as boat-repair yards, fishing-fleet bases and marinas—even some port functions—can easily be supplanted by what are thought to be "higher and better uses", such as major commercial projects, residences or offices. Marine businesses are then either forced to relocate to more remote and less valuable territory, or simply disappear.

Industrial waterfront users, especially the larger ones, will remain. As with all public installations, cities have an opportunity in the working waterfront to produce either handsome, unique expressions or dull, uninspiring buildings. There are many instances, some related here, of the successful reuse of old warehouses, terminals, pierhead buildings and other features from the working port. The Victoria & Alfred Waterfront in Cape Town at its Pierhead Precinct is one among many examples (see pp. 56–7).

In the case of the small marine business, a more complicated decision is whether to intervene to preserve them as the "new" waterfront expands. The working waterfront, while not as dramatic as the major commercial transformations or new cultural and recreational facilities, does provide much-needed blue-collar jobs while at the same time preserving the maritime traditions of a community.

What we show here are examples of working waterfront and transportation installations that are outstandingly beautiful. They constitute an argument not only for keeping the industrial, working waterfront within the city, but for the positive impact a well-designed industrial installation can have on the architectural heritage of that city.

Taken together, these cases make an eloquent statement in favor of planners and developers who, in the rush to make over urban waterfronts, are still cognizant of the vitality and stimulus—economic, social and visual—that today's working waterfront represents, and of those who treat these areas with the respect they deserve.

Right and left, the streets take you waterward. Its extreme downtown battery, where the noble mole is washed by waves, and cooled by breezes, which a few hours previous were out of sight of land. Look at the crowds of water-gazers there.

Herman Melville, *Moby Dick*, 1850

OPPOSITE: **The office and terminal of Coastal Cement Corporation on Boston's waterfront combines efficient function—the offloading of freighters—with sculptural form (see p. 188).**

See these projects in the Gazetteer:

HARUMI PASSENGER SHIP TERMINAL

Tokyo,
JAPAN

project name	Harumi Passenger Ship Terminal
water body	Tokyo Bay Inner Harbor
size	25,723 square meters
cost	$103 million
completion date	1991
sponsor	Bureau of Port and Harbor, Tokyo Metropolitan Government
designers	Minoru Takeyama Architect and U/A
contact person	Masakatsu Honma
	Bureau of Port and Harbor
	Tokyo Metropolitan Government Office
	26th Floor, 2nd Tower
	2-8-1 Nishishinjuku, 2-chome
	Shinjuku-ku, Tokyo 163-01
	Japan
	Tel. 81 3 5320 5548 Fax 81 3 5388 1576

The new Harumi Passenger Ship Terminal on Tokyo Harbor; the main vessel entrance is at left.

Built in 1991 to handle growing passenger ship traffic, the new Port of Tokyo Passenger Ship Terminal is a triumphant beginning of a planned transformation of the landfill precinct known as Harumi. This section of the Tokyo harbor is targeted to become an international center of offices and hotels.

A stunning yet practical six-story structure, the Harumi terminal accomplishes something rare for a transportation facility—a sense of romance. Located a short distance from the heart of Tokyo (only three kilometers from the Ginza district) and accessible by bus and ferry, the terminal is already a favorite spot for visitors of all ages.

Architect Minoru Takeyama explains that the intent was to create a waterfront park at the base of the terminal. This has been done beautifully, using colorful tiles in a bold pattern, water features and successfully incorporating an earlier adjoining public park, a rare section of open space in the industrial Tokyo Harbor.

The Harumi Terminal is completely open to the public. The ground-level deck has a cafe, and the upper levels contain the passenger waiting room, an observation deck at the third level, and a restaurant on the fifth floor. The views from all levels, which take in the entrance into the inner area of Tokyo Harbor, are spectacular. Nearby is "Rainbow Bridge," named for the multicolored lights that line it. A distinctive feature of the terminal is an electric sign advising ships of the direction of traffic flow.

With its striking design, a white structural envelope with bright red accents capped by a pyramid shape, the Harumi Passenger Ship Terminal is a new

LEFT: **An upper deck of the terminal features an observation platform and an elevator to the fifth-floor restaurant, left.**

BELOW: **A landscaped public park near the terminal has been incorporated into the scheme.**

RIGHT: **A front view from the harbor shows the tiled pattern of the lower level plaza. A cafe is located on the first level.**

LEFT: **The new terminal is surrounded by cruise ships and commercial vessels. Across the harbor is downtown Tokyo.**

landmark for the changing Tokyo Harbor. It does the job of loading passengers onto and off vessels efficiently, but is able to accomplish much more as well. It creates a welcoming public space in a harbor that traditionally has been allocated to industry, fishing and flood protection. This is no longer its sole function, and the popularity of the Harumi terminal is evidence for residents and visitors that the initiative has been well worth the effort.

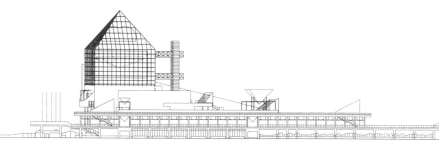

174

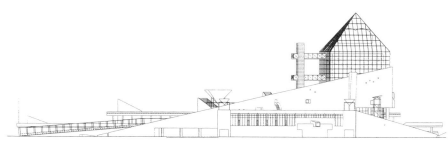

TOP: The east elevation shows the passenger vessel dock in the foreground.

ABOVE: The west elevation is the perspective as seen from the public park that adjoins the Harumi Terminal.

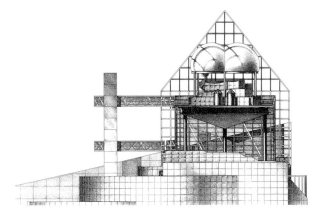

LEFT: Entry points, the restaurant space inside the triangular roof, and the observation and gallery space above it on the sixth level are visible in the section.

RIGHT: The Harumi Terminal, with a vessel docked at right. The tower signals incoming ships about harbor traffic conditions.

OPPOSITE: **The interior of the fifth-floor restaurant,
surrounded by tall windows on three sides,
provides excellent harbor views.**

LEFT AND BELOW: **Sculptures in a reflecting pool
outside the building represent wind, water
and fog and mirror the forms of the terminal
and traffic-signal tower.**

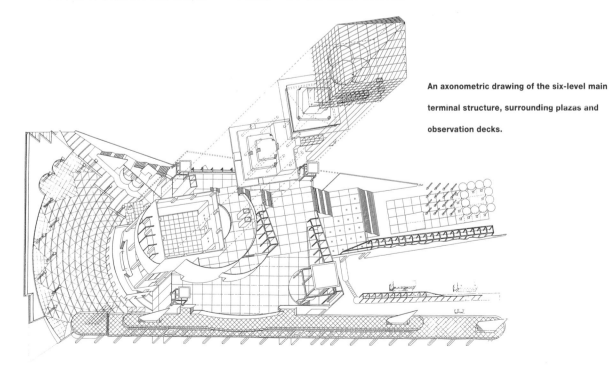

**An axonometric drawing of the six-level main
terminal structure, surrounding plazas and
observation decks.**

BERTH 30 CONTAINER TERMINAL

Oakland,
California, *USA*

project name	Berth 30 Container Terminal
water body	San Francisco Bay
size	34 acres
cost	$78 million
completion date	1994
sponsor	Port of Oakland
designers	Jordan Woodman Dobson (JWD)
contact person	Sara Anne Towery
	JWD
	3664 Grand Avenue
	Oakland, CA 94610
	USA
	Tel.1 510 832 5466 Fax 1 510 835 3464

The curvilinear two-story control and observation room is at the heart of the 15,000-square-foot Administrative Building.

A thirty-four-acre site amid Oakland's busy port, which basically functions as an operating yard for containers and their storage, has been transformed with the construction of three white office and support buildings.

What are generally mundane, nondescript structures, or worse, have been designed by Oakland architects Jordan Woodman Dobson to provide an elegant new presence in the port. The porcelain-coated, metal-clad Administration Building, with cantilevered glass-enclosed ends, is an especially beautiful and functional building. It is elevated to bridge truck entry/exit lanes, conserving space and making it visible to passersby along Seventh Street. Views of the operational lot are enhanced for control personnel and visitors.

The other two structures, the Marine Operations Building at dockside, and the Maintenance and Repair Building, are also white but are made of painted concrete. The maintenance building is linked to the administrative office by an overhead walkway. Functionally, the terminal regulates and handles the flow of containers to and from the Far East in a highly automated, video-controlled export and import operation.

179

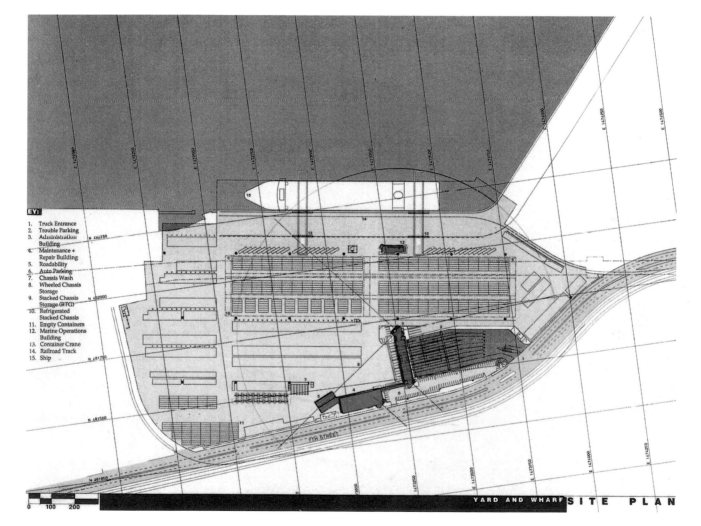

KEY:

1. Truck Entrance
2. Trouble Parking
3. Administration
   Building
4. Maintenance +
   Repair Building
5. Roadability
6. Auto Parking
7. Chassis Wash
8. Wheeled Chassis
   Storage
9. Stacked Chassis
   Storage (RTG)
10. Refrigerated
    Stacked Chassis
11. Empty Containers
12. Marine Operations
    Building
13. Container Crane
14. Railroad Track
15. Ship

0   100   200

YARD AND WHARF SITE PLAN

The project, jointly developed by the Port of Oakland and Mitsui OSK Lines (MOL), had to overcome site challenges. Contaminated material was found in moving 350,000 cubic yards of dredged and excavated earth, and a subway line runs directly under the site, affecting the layout and fill material. These problems were addressed, and a creative solution

was also found for a 1910 switching tower on the site, which is now a museum at nearby Port View Park.

The Berth 30 Terminal sets a high standard for industrial port architecture. It demonstrates that functionality and beauty need not be mutually exclusive, even in the grittiest of industrial settings.

The overall site plan shows the truck entrance from the road, at right, and the lanes leading under the Administrative Building and onto the dock loading area and maintenance/repair building at left.

RIGHT: **A sketch of the Administrative Building
(running top to bottom of plan) connected by
overhead walkway to the maintenance facility
at lower left.**

BELOW AND OPPOSITE: **The exposed steel stairs,
along with the truss bridge between the buildings,
echo the structure of the container cranes.**

BELOW RIGHT: **The porcelain-coated, metal-clad
exterior of the Administrative Building has
metal grates above the windows for shade.**

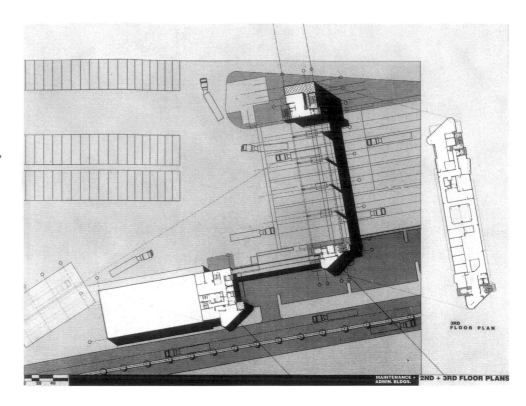

3RD
FLOOR PLAN

MAINTENANCE +
ADMIN. BLDGS. | 2ND + 3RD FLOOR PLANS

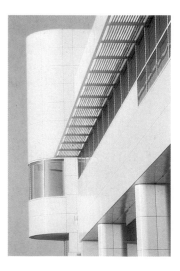

LEFT AND ABOVE: **The Administrative Building's
cantilevered, curvilinear form is visible from
the street. The bridge at left connects to the
maintenance facility.**

OPPOSITE: **The Administrative Building's operation
and function room, used for monitoring truck
traffic, is a dramatic space that allows for
unobstructed views of the surrounding area.**

HAMBURG FERRY TERMINAL

Hamburg,
GERMANY

project name	Hamburg Ferry Terminal
water body	River Elbe
size	12,000 square meters
cost	$19.3 million
completion date	1990–92
sponsor	City of Hamburg
designers	Alsop and Störmer/William Alsop Architects
contact person	Lizzie Nelstrop
	Alsop and Störmer
	Albert Bridge House
	127 Albert Bridge Road
	London SW11 4PL
	UK
	Tel. 44 171 978 7878 Fax 44 171 978 7879

In all parts of the world, modern shipping operations have relocated away from traditional sites, which were often in the center of the city. Such is the case in Hamburg. Although many significant port facilities are still relatively close to the central business district, many operations were moved down the Elbe River, and by the 1980s had left behind vacant properties, forcing the city of Hamburg to develop new uses.

The Hamburg Ferry and Cruise Terminal and Office Building is part of that transition. Located slightly downriver from the city center, this six-level building is a significant new presence on the waterfront. It serves the fleet that runs between Germany and England as well as Scandinavian cruise ships.

The architectural team for the terminal, chosen in a design competition, was Alsop & Störmer of London, working with the Hamburg firm of me di um Architects and Ove Arup & Partners, structural engineers. A third phase, still in the planning stage, would make the structure five hundred meters long, the longest office building in Europe.

The present building was completed in April 1992. Its distinctive A-shape of concrete-and-steel construction, which is revealed through extensive use of glass, mimics the nearby harbor cranes and the industrial architecture of the port. Maritime themes are also reflected in such building details as the viewing gallery supports and adjustable sun visors.

The building sits horizontally along the river. At one end of the first level are the ferry passenger operations, and the remainder of the floor is used for office space and a restaurant. The top two floors over the eastern half of the building, which offer stunning harbor views, are devoted to speculative office space. A publicly accessible walkway extends the length of the second level and has a distinctive, nautical aspect.

The six-level Hamburg Ferry Terminal on the River Elbe.

ABOVE: The concrete-and-steel structure reflects the industrial architecture of the port. The terminal serves the fleet running between Germany and England, as well as Scandinavian cruise ships.

RIGHT: The top two floors of the ferry and cruise terminal facility were built as speculative office space. A third phase of construction will make this the longest office building in Europe.

OPPOSITE: **Office space built with an exposed, pylon-supported structural frame provides dramatic views of Hamburg and the harbor.**

ABOVE: **A section of the building housing customs, police, a waiting hall and a ticket counter for ferries and cruise vessels.**

RIGHT: **The top floors of the structure reserved for office space exhibit industrial detailing.**

BALTIMORE, MARYLAND
USA
Inner Harbor

A classic urban waterfront transformation of its time, the Inner Harbor of Baltimore has been studied by planners, developers and academics around the world because of its stunning success (see p. 14). What was once a collection of derelict piers next to a moribund central business district has, over thirty years (the initial waterfront plan was drawn up in 1964), become a rich and diverse scheme with attractions and activities centering on a tiny water body and accessed by a thirty-five-foot-wide brick promenade.

water body	Baltimore Inner Harbor
size	95 acres
project type	major transformation, mixed-use
cost	$2.5 billion+
completion date	1964– (project); 1975 (promenade)
sponsor	Baltimore Development Corp.
designers	Wallace Roberts Todd, Philadelphia (master plan, 1964)
contact person	Honora Freeman
	Baltimore Development Corp.
	36 S. Charles St., Suite 1600
	Baltimore, MD 21201 USA
	Tel. 1 410 837 9305

BOSTON, MASSACHUSETTS
USA
Coastal Cement Corporation Terminal
Boston Marine Industrial Park

This is a striking industrial installation—a cement loading facility that has an almost sculptural feel. Color is a unifying element: red accents on the four silos are picked up in the pink-and-red two-story office. A street-end park has been carved out beside the terminal on Boston Harbor, so visitors can enjoy the waterfront even while cement freighters unload nearby. The scheme was the result of a collaboration between the cement firm and the city.

water body	Boston Harbor
size	32,000 square feet
project type	working waterfront
cost	$8 million
completion date	1988
sponsor	Coastal Cement Corp.
designers	HMFH Architects Inc., Cambridge, Massachusetts
contact person	Robert Peckham
	Coastal Cement Corp.
	Boston Marine Industrial Park
	36 Drydock Ave.
	Boston, MA 02210
	USA
	Tel. 1 617 635 3342

BOSTON, MASSACHUSETTS
USA
Columbia Point Housing Project

Now a mixed-income community built on a fifty-acre site south of downtown Boston and enjoying spectacular views of the city and its harbor, Columbia Point began as a discredited public housing project. By 1983 most units in the project had been abandoned. A private developer has completely transformed the site in a new layout that focuses on the waterfront in a style that reflects its New England context. The result is a racially and economically mixed community (approximately 400 units for low-income families, 900 at market rate), living in apparent harmony, which is not an everyday occurrence in the US or elsewhere.

water body	Boston Harbor
size	50 acres
project type	residential
cost	$200 million
completion date	1990
sponsor	Corcoran, Jennison Co., Inc.
designers	Goody, Clancy & Associates
contact person	Joan Goody
	Goody Clancy & Associates
	334 Boylston St.
	Boston, MA 02116
	USA
	Tel. 1 617 262 2760
	Fax 1 617 262 9512

CHARLESTON, SOUTH CAROLINA
USA
Charleston Waterfront Park

If historic Charleston is a small city jewel, Charleston Waterfront Park, adjoining the historic district, is a three-acre gem. The planning of the scheme, a collaboration between skilled landscape architects and a knowledge-able mayor, has resulted in beautiful detailing and a perfect fit with the city. A curving promenade runs beside a retained marsh, and the park's landscaped "rooms" have seats under a canopy of trees. There is also a fishing pier. The project was engineered to withstand hurricanes, a design feature that was put to the test even before the park opened to the public. One unusual aspect of this public attraction is the $2.5 million in private donations that helped pay for the redevelopment of the twelve-acre site, which was previously derelict and abandoned.

water body	Cooper River/Charleston Bay
size	12 acres
project type	recreation
cost	$13.5 million
completion date	1990
sponsor	City of Charleston, Mayor Joseph Riley and Trident Community Foundation
designers	Sasaki Associates, Inc.
contact person	Stuart Dawson
	Sasaki Associates, Inc.
	64 Pleasant St.
	Watertown, MA 02172 USA
	Tel. 1 617 926 3300
	Fax 1 617 924 2748

CINCINNATI, OHIO
USA
**Bicentennial Commons, Riverwalk
and Gateway**

Completed in June 1988 for the city's bicentennial, this twenty-two-acre park on the Ohio River with its entry gateway and bi-state Riverwalk is one of the more dra-matic transformations of the time. It was previously a downtown industrial wasteland, but the city and its citi-zens rallied to convert the area into a showpiece. The Cincinnati Gateway is a wonderfully imaginative sculp-ture, which is situated at the principal entrance and dis-plays icons of the city's past. The park has an array of attractions, including sports facilities, children's play area, amphitheater and concert tent, as well as a walkway that features an historic time line. The Riverwalk extends across two bridges to the opposite Kentucky shoreline.

water body	Ohio River
size	22 acres
project type	recreation
cost	$22 million
completion date	1988
sponsor	Cincinnati Bicentennial Commission, Inc.
designers	Glaser Associates; M. Paul Friedberg & Partners; Eric Doepke
contact person	Ronald W. Chase
	Cincinnati Recreation Commission
	644 Linn St., Ste. 411
	Cincinnati, OH 45203 USA
	Tel. 1 513 352 4000

DULUTH, MINNESOTA
USA
Downtown Waterfront Redevelopment

The heart of this outstanding waterfront redevelopment is the twelve buildings, mostly industrial warehouses and fishing facilities, that have been restored for various new uses, including retail. They are part of a carefully planned, gradual transformation dating from 1986 that, though largely in place, is still evolving. Among the outstanding features is the allotment of five percent of project costs for the purchase of public art. This effort includes the dramat-ically lit Aerial Life Bridge and the provision of twenty-two interpretive signs throughout the 150-acre site. At the water's edge is the Downtown Lakewalk leading to the S. S. *William A. Irvin*, a floating ore-boat museum. The entire scheme deserves to be better known and studied.

water body	Duluth Harbor
size	150 acres
project type	major transformation
cost	$150 million (as of 1989)
completion date	1986–
sponsor	City of Duluth
designers	Buckhurst Fish Hutton Katz & Jacquemart, New York (master plan)
contact person	Planning Director
	City of Duluth
	409 City Hall
	Duluth, MN 55802
	USA
	Tel.1 218 723 3328
	Fax 1 218 723 3400

189

FORT LAUDERDALE, FLORIDA
USA
Fort Lauderdale Beach Revitalization

To revitalize its Atlantic Ocean beachfront the City of Fort Lauderdale did a courageous thing—it took away parking spaces and relocated them to side streets. In the place of rows of cars is now a two-mile-long undulating white wall, punctuated with gateways to the beach and coordinated with pedestrian crossings. The roadway has been completely rebuilt and landscaped, resulting in the upgrading of neighboring property. An intricate paving pattern was installed, and there is lighting at night for evening strolls. The make-over was part of an effort by the city to improve the image of this section of beachfront, which is more popularly known for the crowds of raucous students that flood the city during spring break.

water body	Atlantic Ocean
size	1.75 miles
project type	recreation
cost	$13.4 million
completion date	1993
sponsor	City of Fort Lauderdale
designers	EDSA
contact person	Martha Lord
	EDSA
	1512 E. Broward Blvd., Ste. 110
	Fort Lauderdale, FL 33301
	USA
	Tel. 1 305 524 3330
	Fax 1 305 524 0177

GALVESTON, TEXAS
USA
The *Elissa*
Galveston Harbor

The story of the recovery of the 1877 barque *Elissa* from the scrap heap and its full restoration as the "Tall Ship of Texas" is inspiring. The impetus for the project came from the Galveston Historical Society, who wanted a vessel to complement the historic preservation work under way on nearby commercial buildings on The Strand. The restoration of the rotting hull took three years, thousands of volunteer hours and millions of dollars. The boat is now moored beside the new Texas Seaport Museum amid a redeveloping waterfront.

water body	Galveston Bay
size	202 feet (overall length)
project type	historic
cost	$4.5 million
completion date	1982
sponsor	Galveston Historical Foundation
designers	Walter Rybka, technical consultant
contact person	Betty Massey
	Galveston Historical Foundation
	2016 The Strand
	Galveston, TX 77550
	USA
	Tel. 1 409 763 0027
	Fax 1 409 765 7851

HALIFAX, NOVA SCOTIA
Canada
Historic Properties/Halifax Sheraton

Historic Properties is a redevelopment entity responsible for carefully restoring a collection of classic wood and stone sheds and warehouses on the central Halifax waterfront. Though a 1960s urban renewal program almost succeeded in tearing the structures down, the restored area is now a top tourist attraction. Containing shops and restaurants, the wooden buildings have distinctive green, red and gray accents, and the stone buildings have been handsomely refurbished. The next-door Sheraton Hotel is a new structure that successfully blends into the historic precinct. Built of an aggregate surface to match the stone warehouses, the low-profile, four-story project shows that a community can successfully negotiate with a chain operation to achieve sympathetic design.

water body	Halifax Harbour
size	4 acres (Privateers Wharf)
project type	historic, mixed-use
cost	Cdn. $45 million (hotel)
completion date	1976–
sponsor	Historic Properties Inc.
designers	Lydon Kynch Architects Ltd. (Hotel)
contact person	Fred Were
	Waterfront Development Corp.
	1751 Lower Water St.
	Halifax Nova Scotia
	Canada
	Tel. 1 902 422 6591
	Fax 1 902 422 7582

LOWELL, MASSACHUSETTS
USA
Heritage State Park

The revival of downtown Lowell and its splendid stock of industrial and commercial buildings began in the 1960s. After blocking the urban renewal approach that leveled many other declining neighborhoods, the city in 1972 adopted the concept of a national park. A Lowell Historic Canal District Commission was established in 1975, a plan prepared, and park and historic district designations were signed in 1978. Aided in the beginning by low-interest loans, the project has inspired an enormous investment, public and private, in rehabilitating mills, canals and commercial buildings. The effort celebrates the town's industrial past, which dates from the early nineteenth century when English textile technology was applied in Lowell's factories. The mills used water power from a thirty-foot drop in the Merrimack River to drive the first looms. Later there was an influx of immigrant labor and, finally, the industry declined after World War II. The story is told through pieces of public art and in the Boott Cotton Mills Museum, which is housed in an 1835 factory that once employed 2,200 people, most of whom were young women.

water body	Merrimack and Concord Rivers
size	5.6 miles of canal; 583 acres
project type	historic
cost	$1 billion
completion date	1977–95
sponsor	Lowell Historic Preservation Commission
designers	Brown & Rowe, Boston; CBT, Boston, and others
contact person	Peter Aucella Lowell Historic Preservation Commission 22 Merrimack St., Ste. 310 Lowell, MA 01852 USA Tel. 1 508 458 7653 Fax 1 508 458 9502

MAR DEL PLATA
Argentina
Mar del Plata Aquarium

Carved from the coastal precinct of a still-functioning naval base, the Mar del Plata Aquarium is a multifaceted entertainment/educational complex. The project is located immediately south of one of Argentina's leading resorts, and the design is distinguished by careful siting on a coastal bluff, a low-lying profile and use of natural vegetation. In addition to the modest-sized aquarium, there is a shop, entertainment site, cafe and restaurant, children's playground, special events plaza, dolphin pool and water-skiing lake. Paths lead to the shore, where a pool for seals is planned. Opened in 1993, the facility receives 500,000 visitors a year.

water body	Atlantic Ocean
size	96,700 square meters
project type	cultural, educational
cost	$15 million
completion date	1993
sponsor	S. Tutundjian
designers	Mariani/Perez Maraviglia Arquitectos
contact	Mariani/Perez Maraviglia Arquitectos Bernardo de Irigoyen 3017 7600 Mar del Plata Argentina Tel. 54 23 519 836

MIAMI, FLORIDA
USA
Bayside Marketplace

The festival marketplace Bayside may be the best of the newly built installations by designers Ben and Jane Thompson and developer James Rouse. In the now often-imitated pattern, there are twin buildings with shed-like metal roofs. To reflect the tropical climate, the long, two-story structures are white and pastel-colored, with blue-tile accents. There is a wide walkway along an adjoining marina and two-level seating areas and cafes open to the water. Adjacent and to the south is a large park with an amphitheater, and there is a parking structure to the east. Large landscaped areas serve to screen the project and provide shade. Bayside has proved a popular attraction in downtown Miami at night, which is something of a feat.

191

water body	Biscayne Bay
size	20 acres
project type	commercial
cost	$93 million
completion date	1987
sponsor	Bayside Center Ltd./Rouse Miami, Inc.; The Rouse Co.
designers	Benjamin Thompson & Associates, Cambridge, Massachusetts
contact	Bayside Miamarina at NE 4th St. Miami FL 33132 USA Tel. 1 305 577 3344

MONTREAL
Canada
Le Vieux Port de Montreal

Beginning with the restoration of the Lachine Canal lock, the redevelopment of the 131-acre Old Port area of downtown Montreal proceeded according to a plan developed in 1992. Prepared by the Old Port Corporation, the plan reflects extensive public consultation held in 1985. The result is an emphasis on retained industrial structures, expanded recreational boating opportunities, open public space, the establishment of lively attractions and references to local history. Under a comprehensive planning exercise, the nearby Expo Islands are also being developed into a major recreational asset for the city.

water body	St. Lawrence River/Lachine Canal
size	131 acres
project type	historic
cost	Cdn. $65 million
completion date	1992
sponsor	Old Port of Montreal Corp., Inc.
designers	Groupe Cardinal Hardy, Architects
contact person	Aurele Cardinal
	Groupe Cardinal Hardy, Architects
	460 Paul St. East, Ste. 330
	Montreal, Quebec H2Y 2E2
	Canada
	Tel. 1 514 844 1818
	Fax 1 514 844 4595

NEW YORK, NEW YORK
USA
Battery Park City

Battery Park City is a still unfolding transformation of a landfill created in 1976 when excavation material from the World Trade Center was dumped into the Hudson, an action not possible today. After several abortive plans, a scheme finally won favor in 1979. Now substantially completed, its hallmark is the integration of the new precinct with nearby lower Manhattan. Not only does the plan extend existing streets across West Street into the newly developed area, but the design guidelines carry over cornice lines, materials and spacing from established neighborhoods. The project has been executed by the Battery Park City Authority to generally favorable reviews. While the World Financial Center, with its glass-enclosed Winter Garden, is the dominant single structure, apartment towers are the major use (forty-two percent of the total space). Public spaces, such as the wide Hudson River walkway, are exemplary, and recent park additions demonstrate excellence in public design. A new high school is an unusual feature.

water body	Hudson River
size	92 acres
project type	major transformation
cost	$4 billion (estimated total)
completion date	1980–
sponsor	Battery Park City Authority
designers	Alexander Cooper, Cooper Robertson & Partners (master plan)
	Stanton Eckstut, Ehrenkrantz Eckstut & Whitelaw (master plan)
	Cesar Pelli (World Financial Center)
contact person	Phillip R. Pitruzzelo
	Battery Park City Authority
	World Financial Center, 18th Floor
	New York, NY 10281
	USA
	Tel. 1 212 416 5300

NEW YORK, NEW YORK
USA
Ellis Island Museum of Immigration

The magnificent Main Building, which was the point of arrival for millions of European immigrants to the US, was carefully and faithfully restored as a bicentennial memorial in 1990. The French Renaissance-style brick structure, with limestone, terra cotta and granite accents, was abandoned in 1954, but in its first twenty-four years the building had taken in seventy-one percent of all immigrants to the United States. The dramatic space of the Registry Room on the second floor, where new arrivals waited to be interviewed, has been re-created. As in its early days, access to the island is by ferry boat from Manhattan. Efforts to make permanent a temporary construction bridge have been defeated, at least for the time being. Two ancillary structures were also restored in the $156-million effort, but other buildings at Ellis Island remain untouched.

water body	New York Harbor
size	220,415 square feet
project type	historic
cost	$156 million
completion date	1990
sponsor	Statue of Liberty/Ellis Island Foundation
designers	Beyer Blinder Belle
	Notter Finegold+Alexander
contact person	Michael Alderstein
	National Park Service
	Office of Urban Projects
	26 Wall St.
	New York, NY 10005
	USA
	Tel. 1 212 264 8711

PITTSBURGH, PENNSYLVANIA
USA
Station Square

Dating from 1976, this project, a former rail yard that has been turned into a major public attraction, is one of the oldest waterfront make-overs in the US. Five old railroad buildings have been restored, among them the Pittsburgh & Lake Erie Railroad Station, which now features the stunning Grand Concourse restaurant and offices. A former train shed now houses a marketplace with sixty-five shops and restaurants. A new hotel is located here, as is the dock of the Gateway Clipper fleet, one of the largest cruise vessel operations in America. A walkway now in place will be extended to incorporate industrial artifacts from Pittsburgh's heyday as a steel center. When the project is complete, forty acres along the Monongahela River will have been transformed.

water body	Monongahela River
size	52 acres
project type	historic, mixed-use
cost	$104.3 million (Phase I)
completion date	1992 (Phase I)
sponsor	Pittsburgh History & Landmarks Foundation
designers	Landmarks Design Associates, Pittsburgh (master plan); Ehrenkrantz & Eckstut, New York (Phase II)
contact person	Arthur Zeigler, Walter Kidney Pittsburgh History & Landmarks Foundation One Station Square, Ste. 450 Pittsburgh, PA 15219-1170 USA Tel. 1 412 471 5808 Fax 1 412 471 1633

PORTLAND, OREGON
USA
Japanese American Historical Plaza

Located across from the traditional Japanese section of the city, the Japanese American Historical Plaza occupies a small segment (1.65 acres) of the riverfront park created in downtown Portland when an expressway was removed. It was built to commemorate the internment of Japanese Americans during World War II, when families were uprooted and imprisoned in remote camps. Through the artful placement of granite stones, each with an inscription, a contemplative mood is established beside a busy riverside walkway lined with cherry trees. A graceful berm subtly separates the park from the walk. Two large columns form a gateway from the Japan Town area, and a pathway leads to the river.

water body	Willamette River
size	1.65 acres
project type	cultural
cost	$500,000
completion date	1990
sponsor	Oregon Nikkei Endowment
designers	Murase Associates
contact person	Robert Murase Murase Associates 1300 NW Northrup Portland, Oregon 97209 USA Tel. 1 503 242 1477

SAN ANTONIO, TEXAS
USA
Paseo del Rio

There is an important lesson to be learned in the creation of the Paseo del Rio in the heart of San Antonio. Built in the 1930s as a Works Projects Administration scheme that employed hundreds of crafts-people, the resulting riverwalk was lovely but dangerous. Located a level below the city's streets, it became a place to be avoided. The original, 1929, vision of architect Robert Hugman was for the walkway to be lined with shops and cafes, but initially it had none. However, two businessmen in the 1960s campaigned among property owners to make this happen. The result- an intimate water body lined with lively shops, restaurants and dinner boats, as well as quiet spots, all lushly planted—is today the embodiment of the urban waterfront attraction, an inspiration for river-walks everywhere. Details from the original work are exemplary; each bridge design is unique, paving is varied and tile work exquisite.

water body	San Antonio River
size	8,500 square feet (original section)
project type	recreation
cost	$430,000 (in 1940)
completion date	1965
sponsor	City of San Antonio
designers	Robert H. H. Hugman
contact person	Richard Hurd Dept. of Parks and Recreation 202 E. Nueva San Antonio, TX 78204 USA Tel. 1 210 299 7862 Fax 1 210 270 4276

SAN JUAN, PUERTO RICO
USA
Paseo de la Princesa

Restored to mark the 500th anniversary of Columbus' discovery of Puerto Rico in 1493, the Paseo de la Princesa is among the world's most romantic waterfront walkways. With lovely brick paving and lush plantings, including royal palm trees, it runs beside and below the early fortifications of Old San Juan and next to the harbor. Beside the walkway is the restored Princesa building, a former prison that is now the tourist office. Along the way there are a restaurant and food carts. Paseo de la Princesa connects the redeveloping San Juan waterfront, a $105-million project, and its cruise-ship docks with El Morro, the sixteenth-century fortress that overlooks the harbor entrance.

water body	San Juan Bay
project type	recreation
cost	$2.8 million
sponsor	Municipality of San Juan
contact person	Juan Vaquer
	San Juan Waterfront Office
	P.O. Box 3633763
	San Juan PR 00936-3767
	USA
	Tel. 1 809 722 4320
	Fax 1 809 725 0611

SANTOS
Brazil
S.O.S. Praias

"Save Our Beach" is a grass-roots citizen's organization in the port city of Santos, near São Paulo, that has accomplished a miraculous cleanup. The story began with a middle-class neighborhood rallying to control the thousands of people who flowed into the beach area every weekend from São Paulo, even while it was polluted and dirty. The effort led to a limit on the number of buses entering the city and to the construction of a remote parking lot. Citizens then approached the leader of S.O.S. Praias, Marilia Rossi Rogerio, and urged her to tackle beach cleanup. The political force of this movement pressured the local government to install collector pipes, hire four hundred beach guards and to install grates on the canals feeding the bay, among other actions. As a measure of the new consciousness here, the wide crescent beach of Santos now has signs documenting its environmental condition.

water body	Santos Harbor
project type	cultural, environmental
contact person	Marilia Rossi Rogerio, president
	S.O. S.
	Av. Vicente de Carvalho, 42/apt. 151
	Cep 11045-501 Santos, São Paulo
	Brazil
	Tel. 55 132 34 1411
	Fax 55 132 32 4621

SEATTLE, WASHINGTON
USA
Fishermen's Terminal

There was considerable resistance at first to the plan to redevelop the terminal serving Seattle's large fishing fleet. Although outmoded, it was comfortable and authentic. The new terminal, which opened in 1988, resulted from close consultation with the fishing community and its neighbors. It has an industrial feel, but there is a restaurant, a fish market and a walkway that overlooks the fleet and features a memorial, the result of a design competition, to those lost at sea.

water body	Salmon Bay
size	25 acres land; 50 acres water
project type	working waterfront
cost	$9.4 million
completion date	1988
sponsor	Port of Seattle
designers	The Bumgardner Architects, Seattle
contact person	Duncan Kelso
	Port of Seattle
	P.O. Box 1209
	Seattle WA 98111
	USA
	Tel. 1 206 728 3266

SEATTLE, WASHINGTON
USA
Lake Union Steam Plant, ZymoGenetics

Creating a research laboratory from a defunct steam plant, as they have done on Lake Union near downtown Seattle, is a feat. Doing it in a cost-effective and architecturally respectful way is remarkable. The plant, built around 1920, housed seven huge oil-fired boilers as a city-owned backup power plant until it ceased operations in 1984. Because it is a landmark building the developers were not allowed to alter certain elements; for instance, they had to maintain the character of the windows while replacing them, and they reinstalled six smokestacks. Lab spaces are at either end of the building, and the center has an open bay and building services. There is a floating walkway along the lake, a boat-launching pier and a restored house that is now a cafe. The final cost for the lab came to $150 per gross square foot—well under the price of new laboratory space.

water body	Lake Union
size	118,000 square feet
project type	historic
cost	$17.5 million
completion date	1994
sponsor	ZymoGenetics
designers	Daly & Associates, Seattle
contact person	John Schwartz
	Daly & Associates, PS
	2025 First Ave., Ste. 400
	Seattle, WA 98121 USA
	Tel. 1 206 728 8063
	Fax 1 206 728 8117

VANCOUVER
Canada
Canada Place

Canada Place combines a hotel, offices, convention center, theater, shops and cruise-ship terminal in a dramatic structure on the central Vancouver waterfront. Built on an old pier, the structure first served as the Canadian pavilion in Expo '86. Its sail-like tensile roof juts into the harbor and has become a signature of the redeveloping Vancouver waterfront. Public walkways ringing the project allow for dramatic harbor views and close-up observation of cruise-ship dockings. Handsome interpretive signage explains the city's maritime history.

water body	Burrard Inlet
size	1.8 million square feet
project type	commercial
cost	Cdn. $365 million
completion date	1986
sponsor	Pan Pacific Development Co.
designers	Zeidler Roberts Partnership,
	Architects, Toronto
contact person	Eberhard Zeidler
	Zeidler Roberts Partnership
	315 Queen St. West
	Toronto Ontario M5V 2X2
	Canada
	Tel. 1 416 596 8300
	Fax 1 416 596 1408

VANCOUVER
Canada
Granville Island Redevelopment

In this government-sponsored make-over of one of the first industrial parks in Canada, dating from 1913, not only is the industrial look and feel of the past retained, but active industry today exists amid a mix of commercial and cultural offerings. Thus, a cement plant, restaurant and art/design school are comfortably juxtaposed. Granville Island's signature is a true farmers' market that serves a nearby residential population. Located near downtown, Granville is also a popular tourist destination, in good part because it has an authentic feel. The architectural intervention is low-key and reflects the industrial heritage; for example, a new, upscale hotel has corrugated siding. The handling of the car-pedestrian conflict is exemplary —the two simply flow together informally, without the need for curbing. There are perimeter walkways, restaurants taking advantage of excellent water and city views and a ferry service in small vessels. Granville Island has attracted major attention because of its design approach, which in part was born of the need to retain existing industry because the cost of moving it was prohibitive.

water body	False Creek
size	42 acres
project type	major transformation
cost	Cdn. $70 million
completion date	1979
sponsor	Canada Mortgage & Housing Corp.
designers	Hotson-Bakker Architects
contact person	Norman Hotson
	Hotson-Bakker Architects
	406-611 Alexander St.
	Vancouver, B.C. V6A 1E1
	Canada
	Tel. 1 604 255 1169

AOMORI
Japan
Aomori Memorial Park

Developed in conjunction with its sister port of Hakodate when the ferry service between the two cities of northern Japan was replaced by a traffic tunnel, Aomori Memorial Park features a remodeled ferry and a wide public space anchored by a distinctive triangular office structure at a nearby site. The ferry has been redesigned to accommodate dancing, meetings and ceremonies. The project was financed by the local government and organized by the Aomori Waterfront Development Co. Work began in 1982 in anticipation of the impact of the Seikan Submarine Tunnel, the world's longest, which was finished in 1988.

water body	Tsugaru Strait
size	19.7 hectares
project type	commercial
cost	$38 million
completion date	1982–97
sponsor	City of Aomori/Port of Aomori
contact person	Mr. Harushige Takeuchi
	Harbors and Airport Division
	Dept. of Public Works/Aomori
	Prefectural Government 1-1
	Nagashima 1-chome, Aomori-shi
	Aomori 030-70
	Japan
	Tel. 81 177 34 4401

FUKUOKA CITY
Japan
Nakagawa Riverside Promenade
Bayside Place

Fukuoka, in southern Japan, has taken a number of steps to open up and invigorate its waterfront, both riverside and bay. Of symbolic importance is the construction of a walkway along the Nakagawa River that begins at its terminus at Hakata Bay and continues well into the center of the city, making an important link. In the past the river has divided the city; now it brings different parts together. Along the course are a civic hall, the Fukuoka Prefecture Museum of Art and the historic former prefecture hall. At night, shop lights illuminate the walk. Bayside Place is a type of festival marketplace that is very derivative of American installations and features a small aquarium. Nearby is the redeveloped Hakata Wharf ferry terminal and Momochi Seaside Park, which was built at the site of the Asian-Pacific Exposition in 1989 and includes a history museum.

water body	Nakagawa River /Hakata Bay
size	173 acres (Bayside)
project type	recreation
cost	$5 billion (Bayside)
completion date	March 1989
designers	Hakasa Ksaiyo Kaihat
	Urban Design Consultant Co. Ltd.
contact	Port and Harbor Bureau
	Fukuoka City, 13-13 Sekijo-machi
	Hakata-ku
	Japan
	Tel. 81 92 291 0561

HAIFA
Israel
Southern Beachfront

This project transformed a major section of Haifa's frontage on the Mediterranean Sea into a popular playground. Along the beachfront proper are trim sun shelters grouped in four sections and spaced in alternating patterns. Behind them is a huge curved promenade; attractively paved with a diagonal design and lined with restaurants and pubs, it features curved seating areas facing the sea. A grass amphitheater and pleasant restroom and parking facilities round out the project. The parking is separated from the promenade by berms covered in grass, and entrances are emphasized by rows of palm trees and a series of gates.

water body	Mediterranean Sea
size	500 meters
project type	recreation
cost	$5 million
completion date	1993
sponsor	Haifa Economic Corporation Ltd.
designers	Miller Blum Environmental Planning
	P. Kaufman Architect
contact person	Zvi Miller
	Miller-Blum Environmental Planning
	14 Hatishbi St.
	Haifa 34527 Israel
	Tel. 972 4 339 070
	Fax 972 4 339 980

HAKODATE
Japan
Hakodate Seaport Plaza

The companion to Aomori Memorial Park, the Hakodate Seaport Plaza is likewise a redevelopment of a ferry landing that had been deserted as a consequence of the construction of the new tunnel connecting these two northern Japanese cities. The plan here involves the installation of a marketplace in a remodeled ferry shed, which has been connected to a permanently docked ferry vessel, the *Mashu-Maru*, now refurbished to house a museum of local history, as well as restaurants and shopping. There are plans for more recreation facilities, including a marina that will be built in the once-flourishing shipyard and a science museum at another site.

water body	Tsugaru Strait
size	9,800 square meters
project type	commercial
cost	$3.I million
sponsor	Hakodate City Port Dept.
contact	Hakodate City Port Dept.
	Engineering Dept.
	4-13, Shinomome, Hakodate
	Japan
	Tel. 81 3821 349 000

HIROSHIMA
Japan
Peace Memorial Garden

Ground zero of the atomic bombing of Hiroshima in 1945 was at the juncture of the Tenma and Honkawa rivers. There, at the tip of an island, is the Peace Memorial Garden and the remnants of the only building in the area left standing after the bombing—known as the "A-Bomb Dome." The garden contains shaded areas, walkways along the rivers and a museum. In front of the low glass façade of the main building is a pond and a nearby memorial to those killed in the attack. The Children's Peace Monument, located a short distance from the ground zero marker and decorated with origami cranes that were handmade and placed here by children, is perhaps the most moving tribute.

water body	Tenma and Honkawa rivers
project type	cultural
date	1955
sponsor	Hiroshima City
designers	Kenzo Tange, Associates, Tokyo
	Kimihisa Ogawa, Hiroshima
contact	Kimihisa Ogawa
	901, 4–14 Hashimoto-cho
	Naka-ku
	Hiroshima 730
	Japan
	Tel. 81 82 223 4482
	Fax 81 82 223 4428

HONG KONG
Sha Tin Central Park

Carved out of the middle of one of Hong Kong's new high-rise towns, Sha Tin Central Park serves a population of 500,000. It is a kilometer long, ranging in width from 80 to 120 meters, and contains a variety of gardens, play areas and plazas. There is a traditional walled garden, a "western adventure playground," with equipment and games for teenagers, a south garden complete with waterfall and a main plaza leading on one side to the commercial center of Sha Tin, and on the other to a pedestrian bridge over the Shing Mun River Channel. The distinctive areas within the park provide a sense of intimacy in what is otherwise a large space. A walkway runs the length of the river.

water body	Shing Mun River Channel
size	19 acres
project type	recreation
cost	$7.5 million
completion date	1990
sponsor	Sha Tin New Town Development
	Office
designers	Brian Clouston & Partners, HK Ltd.
contact person	Brian Wong
	Regional Services Dept.
	1 Pai Tau Street
	Sha Tin, New Territories
	Hong Kong
	Tel. 852 2601 8631
	Fax 852 2602 1671

HONG KONG

South Horizons

Ap Lei Chau Island

The population pressure in Hong Kong led planners to this thirty-eight-acre site, which contained a power plant and oil tank "farm." While some power company facilities remain, the area is being completely transformed with thirty-four residential apartment towers, ranging in height from thirty to forty-two stories. Spaces have been carefully arranged to avoid a claustrophobic feel, and there is considerable landscaped open space, with pools, sports courts and club facilities, as well as children's areas. There is also a well-designed perimeter waterfront walkway. Two centrally located commercial centers serve the population of 35,000. The units have from two to four bedrooms, are up to 140 square meters in size and offer dramatic harbor views.

water body	Aberdeen Harbour
size	38 acres
project type	residential
completion date	1995
sponsor	Secan Ltd.
designers	Hsin-Yieh Architects & Associates Ltd.
contact person	Keat Tan
	Hsin-Yieh Architects & Associates, Ltd.
	Suite G6, Provident Centre, Wharf Rd.
	North Point
	Hong Kong
	Tel. 852 2811 3999
	Fax 852 2564 2069

HONG KONG

Tai Po Promenade (Dragon Race Park)

Alongside a high-tech industrial precinct is the Tai Po Promenade, a component of the burgeoning new town of Tai Po in New Territory, Hong Kong. Tai Po is scheduled to house 270,000 people by the end of the 1990s. The walkway features some exceptional details—purple railings, lamp posts and paving—and runs from the main housing estate along a wide bay to a park. There is also a sheltered spectator stand with seating for eight hundred for use during the annual dragon boat race. The entire promenade is landscaped and affords dramatic views of the bay and residential towers.

water body	Tolo Harbour
size	21 acres
project type	recreation
cost	$52 million
completion date	June 1994
sponsor	The Regional Council
designers	Earthasia Ltd.
contact person	Ms. Anita Leung
	Regional Council Department
	Information Division
	17F, 1-3 Pai Tau St.
	Regional Council Building
	Sha Tin, New Territory
	Hong Kong
	Tel. 852 2601 8631
	Fax 852 2602 1671

KOBE

Japan

Harborland

On fifty-seven acres, a former rail freight depot yard was redeveloped between 1987 and 1992 as a major mixed-use project that is now virtually a new city center. There are high-rise apartments, offices and a hotel on the downtown side, a large public space around a former dock and a marketplace in a restored freight shed. A multi-level department store is the mainstay of the shopping, which also includes underground stores. The bayside promenade is paved in a tile mosaic of striking patterns; art installations also add interest.

water body	Osaka Bay
size	57 acres
project type	commercial
cost	$4 billion
completion date	1985–92
sponsor	Port and Harbour Bureau
contact person	Koichi Ikemoto
	Port and Harbour Bureau
	Kobe City Government
	6-1, Kano-cho 6, Chuo-ku
	Kobe 650
	Japan
	Tel. 81 78 331 8181
	Fax 81 78 322 6120

KOBE
Japan
Naka Pier Redevelopment

Naka Pier, located in the center of Kobe, has long served as a base for ferry, excursion and cruise boats. Now there is a new passenger terminal at the pier's end, complete with shops. The multistory white structure, which is slightly vessel-shaped, is a forceful new presence on the inner harbor. The sculptural red Kobe Port Tower, its shape inspired by a traditional Japanese drum, is also on Naka Pier. At 108 meters in height it is a Kobe landmark. Adjoining the site is Meriken Park, a twenty-six-acre landscaped space that features public art and a maritime museum housed in a white-mesh structure.

water body	Osaka Bay
size	39 acres
project type	commercial
completion date	1990–95
sponsor	Port and Harbor Bureau, City of Kobe
contact person	Akio Tsuji
	Port and Harbor Bureau
	Kobe City Government
	6-1, Kano Cho-0, Chuo-ku
	Kobe 650
	Japan
	Tel. 81 78 331 8181
	Fax 81 78 322 6120

KOBE
Japan
Rokko Island

Rokko Island, a 1,432-acre rectangular land mass, is the newest of two huge man-made islands in Kobe harbor. On the perimeter are active port facilities that handle container ships, including the largest vessels, at more than ten different berths. In the center is a new community, linked directly to the mainland by monorail. Planned to house a population of thirty thousand, largely in towers surrounding a town center and plaza, the island answers Kobe's need for expansion room, as the city is hemmed in along the coast by mountains. On the bay side is the Seaside Amusement Park, which features fifty water slides, an ample public plaza, a snack bar and a major ferry terminal.

water body	Osaka Bay
size	1,432 acres
project type	residential
cost	540 billion yen (reclamation)
	700 billion yen (development)
completion date	September 1992
sponsor	Kobe City Development Bureau
designers	Takenaka Corp., Takeshi Sugimoto
contact person	Akio Tsuji
	Port and Harbor Bureau
	Kobe City Government
	6-1, Kano-cho-6, Chuo-ku
	Kobe 650
	Japan
	Tel. 81 78 331 8181
	Fax 81 78 322 6120

KUSHIRO
Japan
Fisherman's Wharf Kushiro Port

During a period of economic decline the decision was taken to build a year-round attraction that would overcome dark winters and encourage tourists. In an abandoned port and freight station, a shopping mall/ferry terminal, which includes a fish market, sports facilities and offices, was built first. Next to it is a glass-domed greenhouse. There is a convention center component and an art museum planned, as well as an environmental museum. Two million visitors now come here annually, a three-fold increase from ten years ago.

water body	Old Kushiro River
size	23 acres:
	16,000 square meters (commercial)
	2,500 square meters (greenhouse)
project type	commercial
cost	$1.2 billion (public and private)
completion date	1989–
sponsor	Kushiro Riverside Development Corp.
contact person	Yutaka Matsubara
	WARRC Waterfront Revitalization
	Research Center
	Barque Shibaura 26-1
	Kaigan 3-chome, Minato-ku 1
	Tokyo 108
	Japan
	Tel. 81 3 5443 5381
	Fax 81 3 5443 5380

KUWAIT CITY
Kuwait
Kuwait Waterfront Project

An unfortunate casualty in the recent Gulf War, during which it suffered bomb damage, the one-time Kuwait Waterfront Project created a linear park on the Arabian Gulf that was to have eventually run thirteen miles. The facilities included miles of public beach, a large swimming club, a "green island," which is a landscaped, round sand construction built in the Gulf, and towers in traditional Arabic forms situated on a promontory near downtown Kuwait. Before the project was undertaken, the beachfront had been cut off by a large highway and strewn with rubble. Extensive walkways, fishing piers and parking, as well as trees, trellises and shade structures were in place before the war.

water body	Arabian Gulf
size	13 miles
project type	recreation
cost	$170 million (first phase)
sponsor	Municipality of Kuwait
designers	Sasaki Associates, Inc.; Sultan; KEO Team
contact person	Vicki Rugo
	Sasaki Associates, Inc.
	64 Pleasant St.
	Watertown, MA 02172 USA
	Tel. 1 617 926 3300
	Fax 1 671 924 2748

NAGOYA
Japan
Nagoya Port Building, Garden Pier

Featuring an observation deck atop sixty-three-meter-high pylons, the distinctive Port Building dominates the public waterfront of Nagoya. Built in 1984, it is part of a major make-over of a central port area into a public recreation and cultural center. The development includes an aquarium, an antarctic museum and a maritime museum, the latter located on the third floor of the Port Building. A bridge with dramatic arches unites the aquarium and Port Building and leads to a large public park, Garden Pier. Active port operations take place beside this public space in an unusual juxtaposition. From the observation deck, views of the harbor and city are unobstructed in all directions.

water body	Inner Port and Horikawa River
size	52 acres
project type	working waterfront
cost	$134 million (aquarium)
	$290 million (garden pier area)
completion date	1984
sponsor	City of Nagoya
	Nagoya Port Authority
contact person	Tsuyosi Takagi
	Planning Dept.
	Nagoya Port Authority
	8-21 Irifune, 1-chome, Minato-ku
	455 Nagoya
	Japan
	Tel. 81 52 654 7910
	Fax 81 52 654 7997

NANAO
Japan
Fisherman's Wharf

In the small city of Nanao on Japan's northern coast, a new project has completely transformed the central waterfront. The two-level market housed within a multi-story structure is industrial in design and feel and features a fish-shaped roof. There is a produce market, with fresh fish available, and a collection of arts-and-crafts shops. The second level contains restaurants and has a skylight at one end. A local museum and a ferry terminal are also located here. Completed in 1991, Fisherman's Wharf is now the site of the city's major festivals and events.

water body	Toyama Bay
size	5,384 square meters
project type	commercial
cost	$1.5 billion
completion date	1991
contact person	Takashi Miyazaki
	258 Banchi, Fuchu machi
	Nanao shi
	Ishikawa ken
	Japan

SINGAPORE
Clarke Quay

Five blocks along the Singapore River have been restored and redeveloped as a cluster of shops, restaurants and entertainment venues. Old warehouses and shop spaces in the area were restored, sympathetic new construction added, and extensive walkways with substantial plantings established. Restaurants are located on the river along North Boat Quay, and there are bars and clubs throughout the area. The project is connected to the classic Boat Quay row (see pp. 122–5) and central Singapore by a riverfront walkway and water ferry. As part of the redeveloping Singapore River, a site across from Clarke Quay has been earmarked for a new development.

water body	Singapore River
size	8.6 acres
project type	commercial
sponsor	DBS Land Ltd. (Clarke Quay Pte. Ltd.)
designers	ELS/Elbasani; Logan; RSP, Singapore; EDAW, San Francisco
contact person	Lyn Hogan
	EDAW, Inc.
	753 Davis St.
	San Francisco, CA 94111 USA
	Tel. 1 415 433 1484
	Fax 1 415 788 4875

SINGAPORE
East Coast Park

The largest park space in crowded Singapore, East Coast Park stretches nine kilometers from the city center. Built on a site that includes 150 acres of reclaimed land, which caused major engineering and landscaping problems, the park is now an important outlet, providing a wide range of facilities, all fronting the Straits of Singapore. There is a sandy beach, swimming lagoon, cycling and jogging tracks, a number of recreational centers, concessionaires with bicycles and boats, restaurants, chalets for overnight visits, a fishing pier and several bird sanctuaries, as well as sections that have been left wild. Overcoming high salinity, the park abounds with shrubs and trees, including rows of coconut trees.

water body	Straits of Singapore
size	370 acres
project type	recreation
completion date	1984
sponsor	Parks and Recreation Department
designers	Mr. Fung Wai Chan, Parks and Recreation Division
contact person	Miss Waheeda Abdul Rahim
	Parks and Recreation Dept.,
	5th Story
	MND Complex Annex B
	7 Maxwell Rd.
	Singapore 0106
	Tel. 65 222 1211
	Fax 65 221 3103

TOKYO
Japan
Takeshiba Pier Redevelopment

The make-over of Takeshiba Pier, expanding the site nearly three times to the current fourteen acres, has resulted in a major new waterfront presence. It sits where the Sumida River enters the harbor, next to the beautiful Hamarikyu Garden. The passenger terminal was thoroughly renovated to better handle its one million users, and four towers erected above it. Built to a height of twenty-one stories and set in pairs on either side of Marine Park, the towers contain a hotel and an office building that are connected by a multistory shopping and restaurant facility; and a health maintenance facility/office complex and another office tower that are joined by a restaurant court. Marine Park in the middle is on two levels and is well landscaped. Takeshiba Pier is a forerunner of the kind of development in store for Tokyo Harbor.

water body	Tokyo Harbor
size	14 acres
project type	major transformation
cost	$177 million
completion date	July 1995
sponsor	Tokyo Metropolitan Government
designers	Niikken Sekkei Inc., Tokyo
contact person	Masakatsu Honma/Ryosuke Komine
	Bureau of Port and Harbor
	Tokyo Metropolitan Government
	26th Floor, 2nd Tower
	2-8-1 Nishishinjuku, Shinjuku-ku
	Tokyo 163-01
	Japan
	Tel. 81 3 5320 5548
	Fax 81 3 5388 1576

TOKYO

Japan

Tokyo Port Wild Bird Park

As with much of the area around Tokyo Bay, this park is built on a landfill. Initially, it was an area of broad shoals and shallow places that was a favorite spot for fishing. Fields of reeds and the tidal flats also attracted many birds. Landfill operations in the 1960s, however, essentially drove away the birds and other wildlife. Fortuitously, development plans were halted and nature reasserted itself—grass sprouted through the fill and ponds developed in depressions. Soon birds, mice and other wildlife reappeared and people began using the area for nature walks. In response to public interest, a tiny wild-bird park was established in one corner of today's facility. Though small, it was successful in attracting birds and in building public support. The city rallied in 1989 with today's sixty-two-acre park, which has three ponds, an ecological garden, a lawn and reed fields. The site is at the tip of a developing stretch of land in the harbor near the city center, to which it presents a pleasant contrast.

water body	Tokyo Harbor
size	62 acres
project type	cultural, environmental
cost	$31 million
completion date	1989
sponsor	Park Division, Port and Harbor Bureau
designers	Urban Design Consultant Co. Ltd. and Japan Wild Bird Foundation
contact person	Kunihiko Matsumoto Marine Parks Secretary Bureau of Port and Harbor Tokyo Metropolitan Government 25th floor, 2nd Tower 2-8-1 Nishishinjuku, 2-chome, Shinjuku-ku Tokyo 163-01 Japan Tel. 81 3 5320 5579 Fax 81 3 5388 1577

TOKYO

Japan

Tokyo Sea Life Park

In a city desperate for open space, Tokyo Sea Life Park provides a hundred-acre natural enclave. Created on a landfill site on Tokyo Bay, it contrasts sharply with Tokyo Disneyland, which is located directly across an inlet. The park contains an aquarium and an ecology center, which has telescopes for watching the waterfowl, and interpretive displays. Nearby, a newly planted forest has 25,000 trees and nearly 200,000 shrubs, as well as ample green open space for picnics.

water body	Tokyo Bay
size	100 acres
project type	cultural
designers	Yoshio Taniguchi and Shinsuke Takamiya, Taniguchi and Associates

ZUSHI

Japan

Zushi Marina Clubhouse

The views from the clubhouse of this sports club are stunning, taking in the Kamakura coast, an island and Mt. Fuji. Occupying a commanding location amid a resort area, the design features two graceful, sloping blue-gray roofs that overlap where two buildings are joined. One building, with a bay frontage of unobstructed glass and a deck outside, contains a swimming pool for members. There is boat storage at the marina next door and condominiums and restaurants in the area.

water body	Yokohama Bay
size	1,248 square meters
project type	commercial
completion date	July 1990
sponsor	Seiyo Kankyo Kaihatsu
designers	Takenaka Corp.
contact person	Seiyo Kankyo Kaihatsu Tokyo Tel. 81 3 3984 5933 Fax 81 3 3984 2238

YOKOHAMA

Japan

Nippon-maru Park, Maritime Museum Dry Dock Restoration Ohako River, Yokohama Bay

Amid the gigantic new city district Minato Mirai 21 (see p. 21) is a cluster of three cultural facilities along one of the bay frontages that serves as a low-key contrast to the nearby office and apartment towers. In front of the three-hundred-meter-high Landmark Tower is a restored dry dock. Carefully renovated, with windows built into the rugged stone walls and multiple doors to allow exploration inside, the dry dock is a reminder of the working harbor that was once here. Another reminder is the *Nippon Maru*, a schooner permanently moored nearby. Facing the ship is a courtyard and the Yokohama Maritime Museum. Dock, vessel and museum are connected by a walkway that rings the bay.

water body	Yokohama Bay
size	13 acres
project type	cultural
completion date	1985–89
sponsor	Mitsubishi Estate Co. Ltd. (dry dock) City of Yokohama
contact person	Tsuneo Mitake City Planning Project Dept. Mitsubishi Estate Co. Ltd. Marunouchi 2-4-1, Chiyoda-ku Tokyo 100 Japan Tel. 81 3 3287 5391 Fax 81 3 3211 7675

AUCKLAND
New Zealand
The Auckland Ferry Building

After nearly seventy years of service, the brick Ferry Terminal in downtown Auckland was seemingly doomed by a new bridge that would eliminate the need for the ferries. By 1980 the building was becoming unsafe: its docks were condemned, its paint peeling, its bells removed and the few remaining ferries relocated. But the city rallied when demolition was proposed, and the Harbour Board entered into a one-hundred-year lease with Challenge Properties to redevelop the terminal. They added a fifth story and placed shops on the first level, with restaurants on the bay side and more restaurant space and offices above, and they carefully restored the handsome Edwardian brick-and-stone façade.

water body	Waiternata Harbour
size	5,000 square meters
project type	historic
cost	NZ $11 million
completion date	1988
sponsor	Auckland Harbour Board
designers	Hewson Morrison (restoration)
contact person	Stewart Kendon
	Challenge Properties Ltd.
	666 Great So. Rd.
	Penrose, Auckland
	New Zealand
	Tel. 64 9 525 9000
	Fax 64 9 525 9911

BRISBANE
Australia
South Bank Parklands

Parklands is on a fifty-acre site directly across the Brisbane River from downtown Brisbane. The converted Expo 1988 site is lush with trees and interior water bodies and contains myriad public attractions; it forms a sharp contrast with the freeway-dominated north bank. A wide promenade runs along the river here and is punctuated with landings and lookouts. Major installations include a rain-forest sanctuary, a butterfly house and an environmental exhibition. Among the facilities remaining from the popular Expo is the the Nepalese Pagoda. There is also a variety of restaurants and shops.

water body	Brisbane River
size	39.5 acres
project type	recreation
completion date	1992
sponsor	South Bank Corporation
contact person	Bruce Derrick
	South Bank Corp., Parklands Division
	Stanley St. Plaza, South Bank
	Brisbane
	Australia
	Tel. 61 7 867 2000
	Fax 61 7 844 9436

GOLD COAST
Australia
Bond University Master Plan

This entirely new campus is set amid 247 acres in the rapidly developing Queensland area. A man-made lake carved from a river is the center of the plan. The main campus walkway that runs between two pylons and under an arched building to the lake forms the principal axis. A cluster of buildings surrounds the lake, which is lined with plantings, and a walkway over a channel marks the outer campus boundary. The structures are concrete and have been painted in a muted color. This together with their green roofs blends nicely with a large expanse of lawn and surrounding pine forest.

water body	man-made lake (created for project)
size	247 acres
project type	cultural, educational
cost	Aus. $94 million
completion date	1989
sponsor	Bond University Management Ltd.
designers	Daryl Jackson Pty Ltd.
contact person	Daryl Jackson
	35 Little Bourke St.
	Melbourne 3000
	Australia
	Tel. 61 3 662 3022
	Fax 61 3 663 5239

HOBART
Australia
Salamanca Arts Centre

The beginning of this restoration and the re-invigoration of old Georgian warehouses facing the Hobart waterfront dates from 1974. The state government wanted to buy the structures at Salamanca and Kelly streets for use as an educational center. The owners proposed a donation scheme to encourage the project, and a Community Arts Centre Foundation was established. The buildings, in sound condition, were acquired by the government in 1976, and an arts-and-crafts studio and gallery were set up, along with retail space. Structural improvements began in the 1980s and a conservation plan was adopted in 1992. Despite a lack of capital, the original vision survived, and the Centre has been a catalyst for both community and commercial enterprises. The Saturday Market here is a Tasmanian mainstay and the Centre a major visitor attraction.

water body	Hobart Harbour
project type	cultural
cost	Aus. $800,000
completion date	1976–
sponsor	Salamanca Arts Centre
contact	Salamanca Arts Centre
	77 Salamanca Place
	Hobart, Tasmania
	Australia
	Tel. 61 02 34 8414

SYDNEY
Australia
Sydney Exhibition Centre
Darling Harbour

The outstanding building of the Darling Harbour development (see pp. 40–3) is the Sydney Exhibition Centre. Facing the principal park of the project, it gracefully houses a massive exhibition space, using a mast-and-cable system that is visible atop the building and gives it its distinctive appearance. The Centre is divided into five equal segments, each white in color with extensive glass sections, a concept that reduces its visual mass. An extensively planted, sloped walkway integrates the building well into the Darling Harbour project.

water body	Pond, Tumbalong Park
size	25,000 square meters
project type	commercial
cost	Aus. $80 million
completion date	1988
sponsor	Darling Harbour Authority, Leighton Constructions
designers	Philip Cox, Richardson Taylor and Partners
contact person	Janet Roderick
	Philip Cox Richardson Taylor and Partners Pty Ltd.
	Civic House, 477-481 Kent St.
	P. O. Box Q193, Queen Victoria Bldg.
	Sydney NSW 2000 Australia
	Tel. 61 2 267 9599
	Fax 61 2 264 5844

WHANGAREI
New Zealand
Town Basin Landscaping

This project is an important step for the small city of Whangarei, on the northern part of North Island, to revitalize its boat harbor. Toward that end a major landscaping scheme was undertaken and a new harborfront building erected. A continuous walkway has been added, which includes a decked portion that extends over the water and a brick pathway that is slightly elevated in parts. Stone walls are used to retain lush plantings, as seating along the walkway and in some sections simply as design elements. Sited between the harbor street and a main street, the project, which was a collaboration between architects, landscape architect and engineers, has effectively given Whangarei an attractive new front door to the community.

water body	Hatea River
size	28,000 square meters
project type	recreation
cost	NZ $6 million
completion date	September 1995
sponsor	Whangarei District Council
designers	Hugh Nicholson, Archetypes Wellington
	Ron Esveld Architects
	Butt Design Ltd., Whangarei
contact person	Ron Esveld
	Ron Esveld Architects
	P. O. Box 300
	Whangarei
	New Zealand
	Tel. 64 9 438 0499
	Fax 64 9 438 7279

BARCELONA
Spain
**Moll de la Fusta,
Old Port and Port Olimpic**

Two of the glories of Barcelona are its sense of design and its generous public realm. These come together in the linked promenades that grace the city's central waterfront. With the shift of port activities to the south, the walls that literally divided the city from its harbor were removed in the mid-1980s. Moll de la Fusta runs beside the harbor, skillfully burying traffic and parking beside and under a wide, landscaped promenade. Distinctive, colorful tiles decorate its benches. A later walkway link connects it to Port Olimpic, which was built for the summer Olympics in 1992 and where there is now a popular new beach and boat harbor. Surrounded by cafes along a generous walkway, the area makes for a lively urban scene where previously there was only industry.

water body	Mediterranean Sea
project type	recreation
completion date	1988
sponsor	Autonomous Port Authority of Barcelona (PAB); City of Barcelona; Olympic Committee 1992
designers	Manuel de Solá-Morales
contact	PAB Port Authority Josep Answelm Clave, 27, Pral. 08002 Barcelona Spain Tel. 34 317 6135 Fax 34 317 4148

BERGEN
Norway
**Radisson SAS Hotel and
Bryggens Museum, Bryggen**

The hotel and adjoining Bryggens Museum were constructed after a fire in 1955 and are principally of brick and wood. The 274-room hotel takes its building form directly from the narrow warehouses of old Bryggen that border the site. It is divided into three distinct buildings—with an atrium in one section, a glass-covered walkway in another—and its zigzag rooflines and overall scale are a sympathetic fit. On the harbor side, historic buildings were reconstructed and connected to the Radisson SAS Hotel by a glass-covered restaurant area.

water body	Byfjord
size	24,000 square meters
project type	commercial
cost	NKr. $40 million
completion date	1982
sponsor	UNI Storebrand Ins. Co. (hotel) Shipowner Erling Dekke Ness University of Bergen (museum)
designers	Oivind Maurseth, architect Instanes A/A, Bergen, engineers
contact person	Oivind Maurseth Arkitektkontoret Maurseth Posatboks 4121 5023 Bergen Norway Tel. 47 5 31 66 60 Fax 47 5 32 89 20

BRISTOL
England
Arnolfini

Arnolfini, located in the heart of Bristol alongside City Docks, is an imaginative contemporary arts center housed in a seven-story former tea warehouse. The organization dates back to 1961, but its move to the current site came in the 1970s and refurbishment ten years later. The program is extensive, including exhibitions, as many as ten annually in three gallery spaces; live productions of theater, dance and performance art; varied educational events, such as lectures and workshops; a movie theater showing films from around the world, and a book shop, cafe and bar on the street level. The cafe provides outdoor tables on the quay in good weather.

205

water body	City Docks
project type	cultural, adaptive reuse
completion date	early 1980s (rehabilitation)
sponsor	Jeremy and Annabel Rees; Peter and Caroline Barker; Arts Council of England; City Council and Investment South West Arts
designers	David Chipperfield, architect Bruce McLean, artist
contact person	Tessa Jackson, director, Arnolfini 16 Narrow Quay Bristol BS1 4QA England, UK Tel. 44 272 299 191 Fax 44 272 253 876

BRISTOL
England
Lloyds Bank

Where St. Augustine's Reach meets the City Docks, part of Bristol's former Floating Harbour, is perhaps the prime spot along the considerable waterfront. Lloyds Bank chose it for its UK headquarters,consolidating scattered London locations. The two buildings—one circular, the other curved—are respectful, low-rise and classical in appearance. In front of the main building is a generous public space, an amphitheater and a ferry stop. Much of Bristol's harbor has been restored and the buildings converted to new uses over time (see p. 205). By taking a low-key design approach, the Lloyds Bank scheme contributes to and does not clash with its environment.

water body	Bristol Harbourside
size	20,000 square meters
project type	commercial
completion date	December 1992
sponsor	Lloyds Bank plc
designers	Ove Arup and Partners
contact person	Hugh Stebbing
	Lloyds Bank plc
	P. O. Box 112 Canons House
	Canons Way
	Bristol BS99 7LB England, UK
	Tel. 44 117 943 4400
	Fax 44 117 943 4133

CADIZ
Spain
**Dry Dock Museum and Restoration
Puerto Real**

The Restauración del Antiguo Dique del Astillero de Puerto Real is at once the preservation of a historic dry dock and a memorial to the shipbuilding tradition that continues today at the port of Cádiz. The shipyard heritage center beside the restored and illuminated dry dock contains a museum and library facility in a former pumphouse and a new clock tower that serves as a beacon. Inside the library are pumps restored to working condition and on display for visitors. Inside the museum is a collection of photographs of the shipyard, some dating from the turn of the century. A bright blue cone atop the library and a red accent pole distinguish the modern, white building. The entire area is landscaped and contains walkways.

water body	Bahía de Cádiz
size	9.5 acres
project type	historic
cost	$4 million
completion date	1991
sponsor	Antonio Sarabia Alvarez-Ude,
	Astilleros Españoles, SA
designers	Juan M. Hernandez de Leon, A.
	Lopera Arazola, Arquitectos
contact person	Antonio Sarabia Alvarez-Ude
	Astilleros Españoles, SA
	Padilla 17 Spain
	Tel. 34 1 435 7840
	Fax 34 1 521 8655

CARDIFF
Wales
Cardiff Bay Inner Harbour

A major undertaking, involving two hundred acres amid a much larger scheme, the Inner Harbour project is dependent upon a barrage. It is meant to create a lake where a tidal bay now exists, and is intended to facilitate a number of planned uses, particularly housing. Thanks to a tunnel under the harbor there is no surface road cutting through the area. Some of the first projects, such as the Techniquest science center, were in place in 1995. NCM Credit Insurance has a new office here as does the Welsh Common Health Services Authority; an opera house is planned. Eventually there are to be six thousand new homes and thirty thousand people working here. In the meantime, nearby historic Buteown (or Tiger Bay) and its commercial district are still suffering from earlier efforts at urban renewal and await refurbishment.

water body	Cardiff Bay
size	2,700 acres
project type	major transformation
cost	£2.4 billion
completion date	1991
sponsor	Cardiff Bay Development Corp.
designers	Benjamin Thompson & Associates,
	Cambridge, Massachusetts
	(master plan)
contact person	D. J. Pickup
	Cardiff Bay Development Corp.
	Baltic House , Mount Stuart Square
	Cardiff CF1 6 DH
	Wales, UK
	Tel. 44 41 222 58 58 58
	Fax 44 41 222 58 59 82

CARDIFF
Wales
Taff Trail
River Taff from Cardiff to Brecon

Running fifty-five miles from its start at Cardiff Bay Inner Harbour, this hiking and biking trail parallels the River Taff through gorges, past castles and along abandoned canal paths and rail lines that once transported coal and iron to the port. After passing through the peaceful Usk Valley, the trail ends at Brecon Beacons, a national park in the market town of Brecon. Brecon is also home to a thirteenth-century cathedral. Along the way, a historic and cultural center, an old ironworks and an engine-house mix with the splendid countryside.

water body	River Taff
size	55 miles
project type	recreation
sponsor	Taff Trail project
contact	The Taff Trail Project
	Groundwork Merthyr and Cynon
	Fedw Hir, Llwydcoed, Aberdare
	Mid-Glamorgan CF44 ODX
	Wales, UK
	Tel. 44 1685 883 880

DUBLIN
Ireland
Custom House Docks
Custom House Quay

Old warehouses beside two interior basins (former docks) on this twenty-three-acre site have given way to a glistening new Financial Services Center and a residential block. Major banks have located offices here and more are pending. Additional developments on the site include a hotel and a retail center, the latter incorporating one of the remaining warehouses. Connections to the adjoining River Liffey will have to contend with heavy truck traffic into the active port nearby. Street and walkway details within the project, such as lamp posts, benches and tree-plantings, are first-rate.

water body	River Liffey
size	23 acres
project type	major transformation
cost	Ir. £250 million
completion date	1987–
sponsor	Custom House Docks Development Authority
designers	Benjamin Thompson & Associates, Cambridge, Massachusetts (master plan)
contact person	Gus MacAmlaigh
	Custom House Docks Development Authority
	Custom House Quay
	Dublin 1 Ireland
	Tel. 353 1 363 122
	Fax 353 1 363 353

DUNDEE
Scotland
Discovery Point

Completed in 1993, Discovery Point is a new visitors' center for northern Scotland. Located on a prominent site beside the River Tay, the center is the focal point for a wider waterfront redevelopment that includes large stores, offices and a future hotel. The building is a domed octagon that recalls the design of beachfront pavilions. Beside it is the restored research ship *Discovery* The center houses exhibitions, an auditorium, a shop and workshop space for the *Discovery*. Conference rooms and class space for children are on the second level. Old stones from a former ferry pier are incorporated into the landscaping, as are iron bollards from a former jute works.

water body	River Tay
project type	cultural
cost	£6 million
completion date	1993
sponsor	Discovery Quay Development Ltd.
designers	The Michael Laird Partnership, Edinburgh
contact person	Nina Finnigan
	Dundee Industrial Heritage Ltd.
	Discovery Point, Discovery Quay
	Dundee DD1 4XA Scotland, UK
	Tel. 44 1382 225 282
	Fax 44 1382 221 612

DÜSSELDORF

Germany

"Am Alten Hafen," Hetjens-Film Museum

This project involves a conversion of the old harbor area of central Düsseldorf into a riverside complex that includes a film museum, apartment/office tower, retail area and residential space. The four-thousand-square-meter museum houses a ceramics collection as well as a film studio and small theater. It is built along a water basin beside the Rhine River. Construction of a tunnel to handle the traffic that ran along the river set the stage for this project (see Rhine Embankment Tunnel, Düsseldorf).

water body	Rhine River
size	4,000 square meters (museum);
	16,000 square meters (project)
project type	cultural
completion date	1993
sponsor	Phillipp Holzmann AG and City of
	Düsseldorf
designers	Albert Speer & Partner,
	Frankfurt/Main (David Elsworth)
	Wenger, Düsseldorf
	Scheingert + Wermuth, Düsseldorf
contact person	Manuela Papadakis
	Albert Speer & Partner GmbH
	Hedderichstr. 108-110
	60596 Frankfurt
	Germany
	Tel. 49 69 605 0110
	Fax 49 69 605 01160

DÜSSELDORF

Germany

Rhine Embankment Tunnel

The City of Düsseldorf took the bold step in the early 1990s of putting a major highway artery below ground. It did so in order to reconnect the historic city center with its river, and likewise to put the public in touch with the new parliament house built at the river's edge after Düsseldorf was made capital of North Rhine-Westphalia. The event that triggered the project was the designation of Düsseldorf as the site for a major national garden exhibition. The road, which carries fifty thousand cars a day, now runs through a two-kilometer tunnel, and there is underground parking for one thousand cars. The new riverbank is extensively landscaped, with two rows of plane trees, and features a wide, stepped promenade to the river's edge.

water body	Rhine River
size	2 kilometers
project type	working waterfront
cost	$340 million
completion date	December 1993
sponsor	City of Düsseldorf
designers	Prof. Niklaus Fritschi (promenade)
	Büro Eller, Maier, Walter (parliament)
contact person	Robert Erben
	City of Düsseldorf Planning Dept.
	Brinckmannstrasse 5
	Düsseldorf D-40200 Germany
	Tel. 49 211 89 96743
	Fax 49 211 89 29081

EXETER

England

Exeter Riverside

The Riverside is at the head of a sixteenth-century canal, where warehouses lined both sides of the city center water body. Typically, the sixteen-acre area had degenerated, and a debate ensued about its future. A design competition led to a scheme that proposed to eliminate traffic from the historic quayside by constructing a striking pedestrian bridge across the river to the opposite bank, where a car park was built. Housing projects were undertaken as a prime generator of funds, and a substantial maritime collection has been established at the canal basin. Where dereliction predominated in the 1970s, a charming quarter has been created that now combines leisure, social, retail and cultural attractions in a well-landscaped and congenial setting.

water body	River Exe
size	16 acres
project type	commercial
completion date	1982
sponsor	Exeter Canal and Quay Trust
designers	Niall Philips Architects, with Urban &
	Economic Development Group
	London; Halliday Meecham (riverside
	housing)
contact person	John Clark
	Exeter City Council
	Civic Centre, Devon
	Exeter EX3 0AJ England, UK
	Tel. 44 1392 265 321
	Fax 44 1392 265 265

GENOVA/GENOA
Italy
Genova Aquarium/Harbor Redevelopment
Genova Inner Harbor

The Oceanic Aquarium, built for the anniversary of Columbus' discovery of America, is at the center of a wide-ranging harbor restoration. Included in the sixty-thousand-square-meter area are other new buildings, as well as a restored cotton warehouse and an historic district. The aquarium is a concrete/steel structure in the shape of a pier that contains fifty exhibit tanks displaying a variety of marine species from around the world. Its research focuses on the Mediterranean Sea.

water body	Ligurian Sea
size	12 acres
	190,000 gross square feet (aquarium)
project type	major transformation
cost	$90 million (aquarium)
completion date	1992
sponsor	Porto Antico di Genova spa.
designers	Renzo Piano Building Workshop (master plan, aquarium exterior)
	Cambridge Seven Associates Cambridge, Massachusetts (aquarium interior and program)
contact person	Renato Picco, president
	Porto Antico de Genova
	Palazzina San Biobatta
	via di Sottoripa, No. 5
	16123 Genova Italy
	Tel. 39 10 248 1205
	Fax 39 10 290 719

GLOUCESTER
England
Historic Gloucester Docks

The restoration and adaptive reuse of the fifteen Victorian brick warehouses that line the basins and canal of the now-outmoded Gloucester harbor began in the mid-1980s. As a boost to the project, the city government moved offices into one of the renovated buildings. There are now several museums, a shopping arcade in a new, glass-enclosed structure, historic vessels and an antiques center. The popular National Waterways Museum tells the story of England's extensvie inland waterway system. The project is under the direction of a single development firm.

water body	River Severn and Canal
size	32 acres
project type	historic
completion date	mid-1980s–
sponsor	Crest Nicholson Properties
contact person	Alyson Sheppard
	Historic Gloucester Docks
	Gloucester Docks Trading Co.
	1 Albion Cottage
	The Docks
	Gloucester GL1 2ER England, UK
	Tel. 44 1452 311 190
	Fax 44 1452 311 899

GRIMSBY
England
Alexander Dock

The refurbishment that has taken place at the central Alexandra Dock in Grimsby encapsulates the "urban success story" theme. In the mid-1980s the situation was not encouraging—the fishing fleet had left, unemployment was at twenty percent and the city's image was low. In restoring vitality to the derelict docks located in the city center the borough council gambled that the economy and civic spirit would rebound. By selectively selling off parcels and reinvesting the money, they have achieved their objective. The opening of the National Fishing Heritage Centre in 1991 marked the turning point. Investments include a superstore and a residential restoration of a flour mill formerly slated for demolition.

water body	Humber River
size	12 acres
project type	commercial
cost	£8.75 million
completion date	1985
sponsor	Great Grimsby Borough Council
designers	National Fishing Heritage Centre
	David Rogotham Ltd., Warwick
	Leisure Solutions of York, Ltd. (exhibits)
contact person	Kevin Withers
	Great Grimsby Borough Council
	Dept. of Leisure and Economic Development
	Municipal Offices, Town Hall Square
	Great Grimsby, S. Humberside DN31 1HU England, UK
	Tel. 44 1472 242 000 ext 1075
	Fax 44 1472 348 327

HAMBURG
Germany
Elbschlucht

The office of the architectural practice von Gerkan, Marg und Partner sits high on a bank overlooking the Elbe River in Hamburg. Directly across the river are the giant cranes of the huge port. Waterfront views can also be enjoyed by patrons of the restaurant that is situated here. The turret on the street has been retained from the old river-house structure. A four-level glass façade curves along the riverside, and a wide patio leads to a walkway that descends part of the way down the hillside.

water body	River Elbe
size	2,000 square meters
project type	commercial
completion date	1990
sponsor	GMP von Gerkan, Marg und Partner
designers	GMP von Gerkan, Marg und Partner
contact person	Bernd Pastuschka
	von Gerkan, Marg und Partner
	Elbehaussee 139
	33763 Hamburg
	Germany
	Tel. 49 40 88 15 10
	Fax 49 40 88 15 11 77

HULL
England
Hull Museum of Transportation

Situated on one of the city's most historic streets alongside the old harbor, which is lined with early homes of prosperous merchants, is the Museum of Transport. The museum is called "Streetlife," and it displays trams, trains and early carriages on two floors. On the River Hull side is the second-floor cafe, which is cantilevered over the riverside pedestrian walkway and provides some of the city's best views of the river. An expansion of the museum, which will double its size, is well under way. River traffic here is still considerable, aided by the barrage where the River Hull joins the River Humber.

water body	River Hull
project type	cultural
sponsor	Hull City Museums and Art Galleries
contact person	S. Goodhand
	Hull City Museums and Art Galleries
	Monument Buildings,
	Queen Victoria St.
	Hull, North Humberside HU1 1EP
	England, UK
	Tel. 44 1482 593 902
	Fax 44 1482 593 710

HUSUM
Germany
City Hall (Rathaus)

An obsolete freight dock on the inner harbor has been transformed with the construction of a new city hall. The project was used to reshape the entire area and includes the addition of a pedestrian bridge over the basin, as well as new housing. City Hall is actually in three components, beautifully placed on a plaza where old rail tracks remain. In one brick section are the city offices. A glass-enclosed art gallery, with three levels of display space around an interior courtyard, joins these offices to more, public, office spaces and a structure that houses the council chambers. Paving details in the public spaces are excellent; in some places old stones have been retained and reused.

water body	Binnenhafen (inner harbor)
size	6.2 million square meters
project type	commercial
cost	DM 14.7 million
completion date	1989
sponsor	City of Husum
designers	Prof. Bernhard Winking
contact person	Stephan Schmick
	Prof. Bernhard Winking, Architekt
	Herrengraben 30
	20459 Hamburg Germany
	Tel. 49 40 33 74 95 30
	Fax 49 40 31 49 53 53

KÖLN/COLOGNE
Germany
Museum Ludwig and Köln Philharmonic

The area between the Rhine River and the Cologne cathedral suffered heavy damage in World War II. In 1976 a competition was held to design a new museum and concert hall for the site. The resulting structure, stepped back from the river in six segments, provides a large public space in front that leads to the riverside and allows an uninterrupted view of the cathedral. This area, with its four other facilities, is now a cultural center for the city . The concert hall seats two thousand, and the museum features three-story exhibition rooms that are arranged in distinct sections for different collections.

water body	Rhine River
size	20,000 square meters
project type	cultural
cost	$20 million
completion date	1986
sponsor	Stadt Köln
	Land Nordrhein-Westfalen
designers	Busmann & Haberer, Köln
contact person	Ingrid Kolb
	Museum Ludwig
	Bischofsgartenstr. 1
	50667 Köln Germany
	Tel. 49 221 221 2886
	Fax 49 221 221 4114

LEEDS
England
Leeds Waterfront (Granary Wharf, The Calls, Design Innovation Centre)

The redeveloping central Leeds waterfront already has a number of significant projects in place, and more are being developed. In addition to new office buildings fronting the River Aire and its canals, there is a unique underground shopping area at Granary Wharf, where a grain warehouse has been converted into a cluster of design studios. The Granary is unusual in that its thirty shops are inside a wharf, with the river running through it. One mile from Granary Wharf, at The Calls, another warehouse now houses stylish restaurants and a hotel. Across the river is a Tetley's Brewery Wharf visitors' center, and downriver is the national armed forces museum, nearly completed in late 1995. The Design Innovation Centre contains twenty-two studios and was a pioneer in the then-unpromising area of The Calls; wooden loading facilities that projected over the river from the original building have been repeated in the conversion but replaced with glass.

water body	River Aire
size	200,000 square feet (Granary Wharf)
	27,000 square feet (The Calls)
project type	major transformation
cost	£20 million+ (Granary Wharf)
	£3 million (The Calls)
completion date	2000 (Granary); 1991 (The Calls)
sponsor	Leeds Canal Basin (Developments)
	Ltd. (Granary)
	Baby Grand Hotel Co. plc (The Calls)
designers	Allen Tod Architects (Design
	Innovation Centre)
	David Clarke Associates (The Calls)
contact person	(Granary Wharf) Len Davies
	Leeds Canal Basin (Developments)
	Ltd.
	Arch Y, Canal Basin
	Leeds LS1 4BR England, UK
	Tel. 44 113 244 9304
	(The Calls) Jonathan Wix
	Baby Grand Hotel Co.
	42 The Calls
	Leeds LS2 7EW England, UK
	Tel. 44 113 244 0099
	Fax 44 113 234 4100

LIVERPOOL
England
Merseyside Maritime Museum

Occupying one of five Victorian brick warehouses on Albert Dock, the center of the redeveloping Liverpool waterfront, is the Merseyside Maritime Museum. Opened to visitors in 1987, though displays were not finished until several years later, it evokes the glory days of the city when Liverpool was the largest port in the world—in 1900 Liverpool was home to ten percent of the world's ships. The maritime park includes two eighteenth-century dry docks, where old vessels are moored. Inside the museum, well-presented exhibits range throughout five floors, and a restaurant is on the top floor. Nearby, the Tate Gallery's Liverpool venue, also occupying a former warehouse, is a major visitor attraction.

211

water body	Liverpool Bay
project type	cultural
cost	£160 million
completion date	1989
sponsor	Merseyside Maritime Museum
designers	Franklin, Stafford Partnerships
contact person	Tony Lynch
	Merseyside Development Corp.
	Royal Liver Building, Pier Head
	Liverpool L3 1JH
	England, UK
	Tel. 44 51 236 6090
	Fax 44 51 227 3174

LONDON
England
Camden Lock
Camden Town

A classic success story of entrepreneurs taking a gamble, of starting with something small and watching it grow, began inauspiciously in 1971. Three businessmen bought a rundown stable and other commercial buildings beside the derelict Camden Lock on Regents Canal. Renting space to crafts vendors began as a way to generate cash. Restaurants followed, refurbishment spread, and today, on a given weekend, the area is jammed. It is one of London's most popular strolling venues, with pedestrian traffic spilling onto Camden High Street. One crucial factor was the defeat of a plan for a highway that would have decimated the area. Its threat, however, enabled the developers to make their initial purchases at a low price.

water body	Regents Canal
size	.75 acre
project type	commercial
cost	£60,000 (approximate)
completion date	1971–
sponsor	Northside Developments Ltd.
contact	Northside Developments Ltd.
	Camden Lock, Chalk Farm Rd.
	London NW1 8AF
	England, UK
	Tel. 44 171 870 8764

LONDON
England
Camley Street Natural Park

Tucked between a busy street and the Regents Canal in an industrial area dominated by gas-holder tanks and nearby St. Pancras Station is this magical nature area. Just 2.2 acres, the former coal yard now is rich with reeds, sedge and trees—the original plantings dating from 1984. The major feature is a pond fed by the canal, which gradually recedes into marsh and then meadow. A nature center building serves as a classroom and youth clubhouse. About ten thousand school children visit each year, but because the site is limited, demand outstrips capacity and bookings are made one year in advance.

water body	Regents Canal
size	2.2 acres
project type	cultural
cost	£910,000
completion date	1985
sponsor	Greater London Council
contact person	Project Manager
	12 Camley St.
	London NW1 ONX
	England, UK
	Tel. 44 171 833 3211

LONDON
England
Coin Street Community Builders

The non-profit Coin Street Community Builders, with responsibility for thirteen acres between the Waterloo and Blackfriars bridges on the south side of the Thames, evolved from a community battle in the 1970s to save itself. Dwindling in population, the area still stoutly resisted an office-block scheme for the then-largest vacant stretch of riverfront. Eventually, the Greater London Council conceded. Today the area is a mixed-use precinct whose centerpiece building, the Oxo Tower Wharf, now Stamford Wharf, was refurbished in 1995 at a cost of £13 million. It contains seventy-six flats, nine cafes and restaurants, offices, exhibition space, a planned Thames River Museum and a rooftop brasserie. Nearby, along the riverside walkway, is Gabriel's Wharf, a colorful crafts area in temporary structures. Coin Street also includes such housing projects as the Mulberry Housing Co-operative (with fifty-six units) and a park, and the Community is at work on improving management of public spaces in the area. The Oxo Tower Wharf refurbishment won high praise from architecture critics.

water body	River Thames
size	13 acres
project type	commercial
cost	£18.9 million
completion date	ongoing
sponsor	Coin Street Community Builders
designers	Lifshutz Davidson Designs (Oxo Tower)
contact person	Iain Tuckett
	Coin Street Community Builders
	99 Upper Ground
	London SE1 9PP England, UK
	Tel. 44 171 620 0544
	Fax 44 171 620 1608

LONDON
England
Docklands

Everything about this undertaking is enormous—the territory stretches for twelve kilometers along the Thames, 8.5 square miles in all. The docks, from St. Katharine's on the west (built in 1828) to East India Dock on the east (1806), cover twenty square kilometers. London Docklands Development Corp. (LDDC) was established in 1981 to quick-start the transformation after abandonment of the docks began in 1967. Armed with enterprise zone benefits, LDDC spawned a rash of construction and refurbishment, which features Europe's tallest tower and nine other buildings in an American-style office park. The project went bankrupt in 1992 but was refinanced in late 1995. Canary Wharf was built with little planning direction; however LDDC is currently developing the Royal Docks with a master plan and design code. The original aim of the Docklands project was to house 115,000 people and generate 200,000 jobs by the start of the new century. Investment to 1995 totalled £8 billion.

water body	Thames River
size	5,500 acres
project type	major transformation
cost	£8 billion+
completion date	1970–
sponsor	London Docklands Development Corp.
designers	Cesar Pelli (Canary Wharf)
contact person	Michael Pickard, chairman London Docklands Development Corp. 191 Marsh Wall London E14 9TJ England, UK Tel. 44 171 512 3000 Fax 44 171 512 0777

LONDON
England
Hay's Galleria

The remodeled Hay's Galleria on the south side of the Thames River, between the London and Tower bridges, is the landmark project of a major office development that covers twenty-seven acres. It began life in 1857 as a wharf built around a dock handling tea clippers and other vessels. After a fire in 1900 it was rebuilt to handle dairy products. It suffered bomb damage in World War II but kept operating and prospered until the 1960s, when it was abandoned. The dock is now bridged over, and the U-shaped structure enclosed in a curved glass arcade that sits atop a handsome steel frame, creating a unique atmosphere for shops, stalls and cafes. The building's river frontage opens to a walkway. While a popular spot with the public, Hay's Galleria contains 300,000 square feet of office space and twenty-eight luxury flats. A playful ship sculpture and fountain dominate the interior, and the HMS *Belfast*, now a museum, is anchored outside.

water body	River Thames
size	300,000 square feet (offices) + retail and apartments
project type	commercial
completion date	1986
sponsor	St. Martin's Property Group Corp. Ltd.
designers	Michael Twigg Brown & Partners
contact person	A. D. Smerdon St. Martins Property Corp. Ltd. Adelaide House, London Bridge London EC4R 9DT England, UK Tel. 44 171 626 3411 Fax 44 171 283 6014

LONDON
England
Storm Water Pumping Station
Isle of Dogs, Docklands

Of all the new construction in the Docklands in general and the Isle of Dogs in particular, a small, colorful installation on what is effectively a side street is perhaps the most exceptional project from a design standpoint. Built to handle the most mundane of functions—the collection and release into the river of storm-water runoff—the building contains underground pumps and a storage tank, and is constructed to withstand earthquakes and terrorist attacks. The exterior, however, features a striking array of colors and forms: green-glazed tiles cover the roof, and flying Chinese eaves sit atop great red columns. The walls are covered in a combination of blue-gray, red and yellow bricks. At the front is a wheel-shaped fan through which gases escape. The building is vivid, whimsical and dramatic. It is a handsome structure built for a function that could have easily prompted a much less inspired design.

water body	Thames River
size	8,000 square meters
project type	working waterfront
cost	£3.5 million
completion date	1988
sponsor	London Docklands Development Corp./Thames Water Authority
designers	John Outram Associates
contact person	Michael Pickard, chairman London Docklands Development Corp. 191 Marsh Wall London E14 9TJ England, UK Tel. 44 171 512 3000 Fax 44 171 512 0777

213

LÜBECK
Germany
Musik- und Kongresshalle

In the middle of the historic seaport that once existed on this island site, a striking white-and-glass concert and conference hall has emerged, its stark shape contrasting with the traditional red-roofed city on both sides. The building is effectively in two parts—a round, glass entrance that is recessed under the rectangular building shape, creating a large public arcade, and the adjoining main concert hall building. A new pedestrian bridge connects a main street of Lübeck with the concert hall arcade. The riverfront at the arcade is heavily planted and there is a wide public plaza.

water body	Trave Harbor
project type	cultural
cost	$3 million
completion date	1994
sponsor	Hansestadt Lübeck, Land Schleswig-Holstein
designers	Truper Gondesen Partner, Lübeck, landscape architect
	GMP von Gerkan, Marg und Partner, Hamburg, architect
	Peter Turpin, artist
contact person	Mr. Teja Truper
	TGP Truper Gondesen Partner
	An der Untertrave 17
	Lübeck 23552, Schleswig-Holstein
	Germany
	Tel. 49 451 798 820
	Fax 49 451 798 2222

MANCHESTER
England
Castlefield Urban Heritage Park

This area of Manchester founded by Romans in A.D. 79 was an abandoned wasteland in the 1970s. There had been a thriving cargo basin surrounded by industry, but the canals and warehouses in the Castlefield area fell empty. A slow regeneration since the '70s has resulted in a significantly restored area along a canal and river network that is now alive with narrow boats. Visitor numbers have gone from zero to 500,000. Major conversions, such as that of the Middle Warehouse to shops, offices and apartments, have taken place, and a railway warehouse has become Granada Studios. There is new construction, such as the Castlefield Hotel and the Castlefield Centre, and a dramatic pedestrian bridge now crosses a canal under massive railway bridges. Castlefield Management Co. was set up in 1992 to maintain and promote the area.

water body	Rochdale and Bridgewater Canals
size	445 acres
project type	historic
cost	£50 million
completion date	1988
sponsor	Castlefield Management Co.
contact person	General Manager
	Castlefield Centre
	101 Liverpool Rd.
	Castlefield, Manchester M3 4JN
	England, UK
	Tel. 44 161 834 4026
	Fax 44 161 839 8747

OSLO
Norway
Aker River Environmental Park

The Aker River, which runs ten kilometers from its source to the Oslo fjord, powered a variety of industries in the nineteenth century. These included sawmills, iron foundries, cotton mills, soap factories and shipyards. When displaced by alternative power sources, the river went into a total decline, becoming polluted and abandoned. A plan developed in 1917 called for a river cleanup and the creation of a public park. Pollution was controlled by 1971 and the walkway originally envisioned is now largely in place. In 1987, a new planning exercise was undertaken that focused on both preserving natural elements and restoring the empty factories for new uses. Buildings at the Bjolsen Dam now house cafes and crafts shops, while a Nature Center occupies another industrial structure and there are now a number of green open spaces.

water body	Aker River
size	10 kilometers
project type	cultural, environmental
cost	NKr. 100 million (approximately)
completion date	1987
designers	Dept. of Parks and Recreation
contact	Dept. of Parks and Recreation
	Oslo
	Norway
	Tel. 47 2 38 18 70

PALMA, MAJORCA

Spain

Restoration of the Rondo Promenade

Running one kilometer in length, the promenade and park here is being reconstructed to provide a new link between the seaside and the old city above. A plan dating from 1983 called for the transformation of a former military area into a public space featuring gardens, an open-air theater, cafes, a naval museum and access to the city above. Part of the work involved stabilizing the ancient city walls, the original fortification. An old underground tunnel that links the city and the sea has been restored and is now lit with a skylight, and a staircase was built from fragments of old stone buildings.

water body	Mediterranean Sea
size	1 kilometer
project type	recreation
cost	$1,752,000
completion date	1983–
sponsor	Ministry of Urbanism and Public Works
designers	José Antonio Martinez Lapena-Elias Torres Tur Arquitectos
contact person	Ramon Felix
	José Antonio Martinez Lapena-Elias Torres Tur
	Roca i Batlle 14
	088023 Barcelona Spain
	Tel. 34 3 212 14 16
	Fax 34 3 418 65 44

PARIS

France

Mémorial des Martyrs de la Déportation Ile de la Cité

Located at the triangular tip of the Ile de la Cité in the shadow of Notre Dame, this monument to French citizens deported by the Nazi regime is a stirring tribute. The work of architect George-Henri Pingusson, the below-grade monument uses stone and metal to create a haunting feel. Stairs descend to a small plaza. The Seine can be viewed through a black-iron grated window in the wall. Up above, there is a stark black iron sculpture. A narrow entry leads to an intimate meditative space. A memorial wall of thousands of clear marbles glows near a coffinlike slab. This underground area is flanked by identical "cells" and walls that bear the names of the Nazi concentration camps. An inscription there reads, *"Pardonne, mais, n'oubliez pas . . ."*

water body	Seine River
project type	cultural
completion date	1962
designers	George-Henri Pingusson, A. Bianchi

ROTTERDAM

The Netherlands

Erasmus Bridge, Kop van Zuid

Under construction in late 1995 is what is destined to become one of the great bridges of the world—the Erasmus Bridge connecting central Rotterdam on the north with Kop van Zuid, a major developing neighborhood on the south. A single Y-shaped tower 139 meters high dominates, holding a sheath of cables to one side, a single pair to the north. When illuminated, it will be a dramatic new presence on the waterfront. For the considerable shipping traffic along the River Maas, there will be a huge steel lift bridge, said to be the largest in the world, that will provide a fifty-meter passage. The symbolism of the bridge is considerable, as it links north Rotterdam with the working-class precincts of the south. Kop van Zuid is one of the world's largest redevelopments with 5,300 housing units planned, 400,000 square meters of office space and 95,000 square meters allotted to retail, sports and entertainment.

water body	River Maas
size	800 meters long
project type	working waterfront, transportation
cost	DFl. 365 million
completion date	mid-1996
sponsor	Kop van Zuid; Rotterdam Public Works Dept.
designers	Ben van Berkel
contact person	Han Hok
	Kop van Zuid
	Stieltjesstraat 21
	3071 JV Rotterdam The Netherlands
	Tel. 31 10 213 01 01
	Fax 31 10 213 00 91

SALFORD
England
Salford Quays

The docklands here, on the Manchester Ship Canal, began a decline after World War II that ended in 1984, when the Salford City Council bought the seventy-five acres for redevelopment. Under a master plan adopted a year later, infrastructure improvements began and housing, office and some retail development burgeoned. In an important step, three of the former docks were sealed off from the polluted ship canal, the fourth left open for a marina. Around the newly aerated water, housing blocks have been built in the middle portion of the project, an office precinct featuring gleaming glass towers is beside the large Erie/Huron Basin to the north, and a commercial concentration is at the southern end. Unfenced walkways are featured throughout. By 1995 Salford Quays was well on its way to achieving its projected goal of employing ten thousand people.

water body	Manchester Ship Canal
size	148 acres
project type	major transformation
cost	£370 million (1990 estimate)
completion date	1986–
sponsor	City of Salford
designers	Shephard, Epstein & Hunter, London (master plan)
	Ove Arup & Partners, London
contact person	W.A.K. Smuthers
	City of Salford
	Chorley Road, Swinton
	Salford M27 2BW England, UK
	Tel. 44 61 793 3743
	Fax 44 61 727 8269

STOCKHOLM
Sweden
Vasa Museum

A major presence today on the Stockholm waterfront is the rugged, industrial brown Vasa Museum. Opened in 1990, it houses a warship that sank on its maiden voyage in 1628 several hundred yards from the dock. Its salvaging from the floor of the harbor in 1956 was an amazing technical feat. Along with the well-preserved vessel came 25,000 other items, many of them boat parts, which have been laboriously sorted and identified. There were more than six hundred sculptures found, which have now been restored to their original places on the vessel. Put in a temporary museum at first, the Vasa became the most visited attraction in Scandinavia. Its new home, with the distinctive three masts through the roof, allows visitors a close inspection. The museum is set by an old dry dock and features an attractive cafe with waterfront views and a shop. Outside, a walkway lines the harbor edge.

water body	Saltsjön
project type	cultural
completion date	1990
sponsor	Vasa Museum
designers	Goran Mansson and Marianne Dahlback
contact person	Lans-Ake Kvarning, director
	Vasa Museum
	P.O. Box 27131
	10252 Stockholm Sweden
	Tel. 46 8 666 4879

STOCKHOLM
Sweden
Stockholm Water Festival

In just five years, the Stockholm Water Festival has built itself into one of Europe's top events, with an estimated four million attending in August 1995 over a ten-day period. The central waterfront is completely taken over by the festival's 1,200 events. Major corporate sponsorship helps underwrite the serious aspects of the festival—an annual Stockholm Water Prize (given last year to Jon Lane, director of WaterAid, London, which helps remote third world areas with water cleanup); and an annual water symposium, conducted simultaneously with the festival. The Water Prize carries an award of $150,000. In 1994 the festival organization combined with others to erect a water treatment plant in Estonia to contribute to a cleaner Baltic Sea.

water body	Stockholm harbor
project type	cultural, environmental
contact	Stockholm Water Festival
	Amiralitetshuset, Skeppsholmen
	S-111 49 Stockholm
	Sweden
	Tel. 46 8 614 3400
	Fax 46 8 679 6465

SUNDERLAND
England
Sunderland Sculpture Project

A small component of the St. Peter's riverside redevelopment, one of the Tyne and Wear Development Corporation's undertakings, is a sculpture project. Gradually appearing on a site next to the new campus of Sunderland University, which is now under development, the sculptures come in a variety of forms and shapes. A resident sculptor, Colin Wilbourn, leads the project team. Among the installations is *Stone Stair Carpet*, sandstone steps, leading to the water from a pier, that are both functional and decorative and recall the local fishing tradition. *Red House* pays homage to the community's shipbuilding tradition. *Watching and Waiting*, a hilltop sculpture featuring a stone picnic hamper and stool and a steel telescope and sea chart, was a collaborative effort that grew from stories of local residents who recalled waiting on the hill for ships to return.

water body	River Wear
size	.5 square kilometer
project type	cultural
cost	£100,000 (annually)
completion date	1991–97
sponsor	Tyne and Wear Development Corp./
	Northern Rock Building Society
designers	Davies Tynedale & Associates
	(university campus)
contact person	Lucy Milton
	Artists Agency
	18 Norfolk St.
	Sunderland SR1 1EA
	England, UK
	Tel. 44 191 510 9318
	Fax 44 191 565 2846

TEESDALE
England
Teeside

A major recreation area has been established along the River Tees in northern England with the construction of a barrage. The massive structure, opened in April 1995, created an eleven-mile stretch of river that is free of pollution. Now visitors engage in a variety of water sports, such as fishing, canoeing, wind-surfing and swimming. Adjoining the barrage is a white-water course, said to be England's largest, which can be adjusted for different levels of competition. Eventually a walkway will run the full length of the river, from its mouth to its point of origin in the Pennine hills; major segments were in place in 1995. A plan for a huge site at Teesdale, near Stockton, with £50 million in development around a series of canals, is being considered by the Teesdale Development Corp. Major office projects, housing, the University College Stockton campus and health facilities will be included.

water body	River Tees
size	11 miles
project type	recreation
cost	£50 million
completion date	1990–95
sponsor	Teeside Development Corp.
designers	Montgomery Watson
	Napper Partnerships
	Ove Arup and Partners (Tees Barrage)
contact person	Duncan Hall, chief executive
	Teeside Development Corp.
	Dunedin House Riverside Quay
	Stockton-on-Tees, Cleveland
	England
	Tel. 44 1642 677 123
	Fax 44 1642 676 123

VENICE
Italy
Mazzorbo Housing Project
Mazzorbo Island

In the magical setting of the Lagoon of Venice are several islands. Mazzorbo is linked to the better-known Burano by a bridge and to Venice by ferry. New housing in the form of twelve clusters of townhouses, three stories in height, have been carefully fitted into the centuries old historic context established by generations of fishing families, artisans and gardeners. Wide stepped walkways provide generous public access to the water's edge.

water body	Lagoon of Venice
project type	residential
completion date	1995
sponsor	Mazzorbo Island
designers	Giancarlo De Carlo
contact person	Giancarlo De Carlo
	via Pier Capponi 13
	20145 Milano
	Italy
	Tel. 39 2 48 01 18 32
	Fax 39 2 48 19 46 67

NOTES TO THE TEXT

INTRODUCTION

[1] Nicholas Falk, "UK Waterside Development," in *Urban Design*, July 1995, p. 19.

[2] Hidenobu Jinnai, *Italian Aquascapes* (Tokyo: Process Architecture Co. Ltd., 1993) p. 221.

[3] *Industrial Culture and Industrial Work in Coastal Areas: How to Handle the Heritage of Port and Shipping History*, publication of conference proceedings (Hamburg: Hans Christians Verlag, 1992) p. 12.

[4] *The New York Times*, July 18, 1995, p. D1.

CHAPTER 2

Southgate

[1] Department of Planning and Development, Government of Victoria, "Central Melbourne: The Development of the City Reaches of the Yarra River," in *Landscape Australia*, March 1986, p. 196.

CHAPTER 3

Sydney Opera House

[1] Anonymous, "Closing the Utzon Chapter," in *The Magazine of the Sydney Opera House*, November, 1980, p. 16.

CHAPTER 4

Boat Quay

[1] Joan Hon, *Tidal Fortunes—A Story of Change: The Singapore River and Kallang Basin* (Landmark Books Pte. Ltd., n.d.) Foreward.

CHAPTER 6

Entrepot West

[1] Anonymous, "On the Waterfront," in *Euro Holland Trade*, January 1994, p. 100.

BOOKS AND PERIODICALS

BOOKS

Alexander, Christopher, *The Timeless Way of Building*, (New York: Oxford University Press, 1979).

Al Naib, S. K., ed., *European Docklands: Past, Present and Future* (London: Thames and Hudson, 1991).

American Boat & Yacht Council, Inc., *Boating Information: A Bibliography and Source List* (Amityville, New York: American Boat & Yacht Council, n.d.).

Appleyard, Donald, *Livable Streets* (Los Angeles and London: University of California Press Berkeley, 1981).

Aslan, Liliana; Joselevich, I.; Novoa, G.; Saiegh, D., and Santalo, A., *Buenos Aires Puerto 1887-1992* (Buenos Aires: IPU Inventario de Patrimonio Urbano, 1992).

Bachelard, Gaston, *Water and Dreams: An Essay On the Imagination of Matter* (Dallas: The Pegasus Foundation Dallas, 1942, 1983).

Baltimore City Planning Department, *The Baltimore Harbor* (Baltimore, Maryland, 1985).

Barnett, Jonathan, *An Introduction to Urban Design* (New York: Harper & Row, 1982).

Barnett, Jonathan, *The Elusive City: Five Centuries of Design, Ambition and Miscalculation* (New York: Harper & Row, 1986).

Breen, Ann and Rigby, Dick, *Caution: Working Waterfront: The Impact of Change on Marine Enterprises* (Washington, D.C.: The Waterfront Press, 1985). Four case studies addressing the clash between growing commercial appreciation for waterfront sites, and traditional marine business.

Breen, Ann and Rigby, Dick, *Fishing Piers: What Cities Can Do* (Washington, D. C.: The Waterfront Press, 1986).

Breen, Ann and Rigby, Dick, eds., *Urban Waterfronts '83 to '88*, varied titles (Washington, D.C.: The Waterfront Press, 1989). Summaries of program content of annual conferences organized by the Waterfront Center. Illustrated.

Breen, Ann and Rigby, Dick, *Waterfronts: Cities Reclaim their Edge* (New York: McGraw-Hill Inc., 1994). Contains 75 cases studies, primarily from North America, chosen by in the first five years of the Waterfront Center's awards program.

Breen Cowey, Ann; Kaye, Robert; O'Conner, Richard and Rigby, Dick, *Improving Your Waterfront: A Practical Guide* (Washington, D.C.: U.S. Department of Commerce/N.O.A.A., 1980). Contains information about specific techniques that communities have used for successful waterfront redevelopment projects.

Bruttomesso, Rinio, ed., *Waterfronts: A New Urban Frontier* (Venice, Italy: Citta d'Acqua, 1991). Proceedings from the conference on waterfront projects around the world held in Venice, Italy, in January 1991.

Buckley, Raymond M., and Walton, James M., *Fishing Piers: Their Design, Operation and Use* (Washington: Sea Grant Communications Seattle, Sea Grant Technical Report WSG-81-1, February 1981).

Buttenwieser, Ann L., *Manhattan Water-Bound: Planning and Developing Manhattan's Waterfront from the Seventeenth Century to the Present* (New York: New York University Press, 1987).

Collins, Richard C.; Waters, Elizabeth B., and Dotson, A. Bruce, *America's Downtowns: Growth, Politics & Preservation* (Washington, D.C.: The Preservation Press, 1991).

Cullen, Gordon, *The Concise Townscape* (New York: Van Nostrand Reinhold, 1961).

de Caceres, Rafael and Ferrer, Montserrat, eds., *Barcelona espacio publico* (Barcelona: Ajuntament de Barcelona, 1992).

Diamonstein, Barbaralee, *Remaking America: New Uses, Old Places* (New York: Crown Publishers, Inc., 1986).

Fischer, Richard, with John Walton, *British Piers* (London: Thames and Hudson Ltd., 1987).

Fitch, James Marston, *Historic Preservation: Curatorial Management of the Built World* (Charlottesville, Virginia, and London: University of Virginia Press, 1990).

Fleming, Ronald Lee and Von Tscharner, Renata, *Placemakers: Creating Public Art that Tells You Where You Are* (New York: Harcourt Brace Jovanovich, 1987).

Fried, Lewis F., *Makers of the City* (Massachusetts: The University of Massachusetts Press Amherst, 1990).

Frieden, Bernard J. and Sagalyn, Lynne B., *Downtown, Inc.: How America Rebuilds Cities* (Cambridge, Massachusetts, and London: The MIT Press, 1990).

Gehl, Jan, *Life Between Buildings—Using Public Space* (New York: Van Nostrand Reinhold Company, 1987). English edition.

Girouard, Mark, *Cities & People*, (New Haven, Connecticut: Yale University Press, 1985).

Glazer, Nathan and Lilla, Mark, eds., *The Public Face of Architecture: Civic Culture and Public Spaces* (New York: The Free Press, A Division of Macmillan, Inc., 1987).

Goode, David and Joseph, Michael, *Wild in London* (London: Shell Books, 1986).

Goodman, Paul and Percival, *Communitas: Means of Livelihood and Ways of Life* (New York: Vintage Books, Random House, 1947, 1960).

Goodman, Robert, *After the Planners* (New York: Simon and Schuster, 1971).

Gourley, Catherine, *Island in the Creek—The Granville Island Story* (Madeira Park, B.C., Canada: Harbour Publishing Co. Ltd., 1988).

Gratz, Roberta Brandes, *The Living City: How Urban Residents Are Revitalizing America's Neighborhoods* (New York: Touchstone, Simon & Schuster, Inc., 1989).

Hackney, Rod, *The Good, the Bad & the Ugly. Crisis in Cities* (London, Sydney, Auckland, Johannesburg: Frederick Muller, 1990).

Halprin, Lawrence, *Cities* (Cambridge, Massachusetts: The MIT Press, 1972.

Hiss, Tony, *The Experience of Place* (New York: Alfred A. Knopf, Inc., 1990).

Hon, Joan, *Tidal Fortunes—A Story of Change: The Singapore River and Kallang Basin* (Singapore: Landmark Books Pte. Ltd., n.d.).

Hough, Michael, *Out of Place: Restoring Identity to the Regional Landscape* (New Haven, Connecticut, and London: Yale University Press, 1990).

Hoyle, B. S.; Pinder, D. A., and Husein, M. S., eds., *Revitalizing the Waterfront: International Dimensions of Dockland Redevelopment* (London: Belhaven Press, 1988).

Hugill, Stan, *Sailortown* (New York: Dalton 1967). Out of print.

Huxtable, Ada Louise, *Architecture, Anyone? Cautionary Tales of the Building Art* (New York: Random House, 1986).

International Symposium on Port Preservation, Sept. 6–9, *Industriekultur und Arbeitswelt an der Wasserkante*, "Industrial Culture and Industrial Work in Coastal Areas" (Hamburg: Hans Christians Verlag, 1991).

Jacobs, Allan B., *Looking at Cities* (Cambridge, Massachusetts, and London: Harvard University Press, 1985).

Jacobs, Jane, *The Death and Life of Great American Cities* (New York: Random House, 1961).

Japan Port and Harbor Association, *Waterfront Redevelopment in Japan* (Tokyo: Technology Transfer Institute, 1979).

Jinnai, Hidenobu, et. al., *Italian Aquascapes* (Tokyo: Process Architecture, Co., Ltd., 1993).

Johnson, David, *The Auckland Ferry Building* (Auckland: Auckland Maritime Museum, 1988).

Kondo, Takeo, *Architectural Rendering: 3 Waterfronts* (Japan: Japan Architectural Renderers Association, 1991).

Konvitz, Josef, W., *Cities and the Sea: Port City Planning in Early Modern Europe* (Baltimore and London: Johns Hopkins University Press, 1978).

Krier, Rob, *Urban Space* (New York: Rizzoli, 1979).

Listokin, David, *Living Cities* (New York: Priority Press Publications, 1985).

Little, Charles E., *Greenways for America* (Baltimore. The Johns Hopkins University Press, 1990).

Lozano, Eduardo, *Community Design and the Culture of Cities* (Cambridge: Cambridge University Press, 1990).

Lynch, Kevin, *The Image of The City* (Cambridge, Massachusetts, and London: The M.I.T. Press, 1960).

Marius, Carol, *Barcelona de Bat a Bat* (Barcelona: Lunwerg Editores S.A., 1993).

McHarg, Ian L., *Design With Nature* (Garden City, New York: The Natural History Press, 1969).

Merrens, Roy, *Urban Waterfront Redevelopment in North America: An Annotated Bibliography* (Downsview, Ontario: University of Toronto/York University, 1980). Transportation Research Report No. 66.

Moore, Arthur Cotton, et al., *Bright Breathing Edges of City Life: Planning for Amenity Benefits of Urban Water Resources*, prepared for Office of Water Resources Research, Department of the Interior (Springfield, Virginia: National Technical Information Service, PB 202 880, 1971). Early study of waterfronts, includes case studies on Washington, D. C., Boston, Buffalo, New Orleans, Louisville and Oakland.

Moore, Charles W., *Water and Architecture* (New York: Harry N. Abrams, 1994).

National Capital Commission, *A Future for our Rivers: A Synopsis of the Conference held in Canada's Capital by the National Capital Commission*, June 8-11, 1987.

Oldenburg, Ray, *The Great Good Place* (New York: Paragon House, 1989).

Phillips, Alan, *The Best in Leisure and Public Architecture* (Switzerland: Rotovision, 1993).

Pudney, John, *London's Docks* (London: Thames and Hudson, 1975).

Relph, Edward, *The Modern Urban Landscape* (Baltimore: Johns Hopkins University Press, 1987).

Rossi, Aldo, *The Architecture of the City* (Cambridge, Massachusetts, and London: The M.I.T. Press, 1982). With introduction by Peter Eisenman.

The Royal Architectural Institute of Canada, *Metropolitan Mutations: The Architecture of Emerging Public Spaces* (London and Toronto: Little, Brown and Company Limited, 1989).

The Royal Commission on the Future of the Toronto Waterfront, *Watershed* (Toronto, Ontario, Interim Report, 1990). A product of the Royal Commission's ambitious publishing program, which includes ten book-length reports, five working papers, five technical papers, the first interim report and eight newsletters.

Sennett, Richard, *The Conscience of the Eye: The Design and Social Life of Cities* (New York: Alfred A. Knopf, 1990).

Simpson, Alister, with Dennis Wilson, *Waterfront Precedents* (Toronto: City of Toronto Planning Board, 1976).

Spirn, Anne Whiston, *The Granite Garden* (New York: Basic Books, Inc., 1984).

Stanford, Joseph M., compiler and ed., *Sea History's Guide to American and Canadian Maritime Museums* (Croton-on-Hudson, New York: Sea History Press, 1990).

Sykes, Jill, *Sydney Opera House From the Outside In* (Sydney: Sydney Opera House Trust, 1993).

Untermann, Richard K., *Accommodating the Pedestrian: Adapting Towns and Neighborhoods for Walking and Bicycling* (New York: Van Nostrand Reinhold Company, 1984).

HRH The Prince of Wales, *A Vision of Britain: A Personal View of Architecture* (London, New York, Toronto: Doubleday, 1989).

Webber, Peter, ed., *The Design of Sydney: Three Decades of Change in the City Centre* (Agincourt, Ontario: The Carswell Co. Ltd.; North Ryde, N.S.W.: The Law Book Company Ltd., 1988).

Wylson, Anthony, *Aquatecture: Architecture and Water* (New York: Van Nostrand Reinhold Company; London: The Architectural Press, 1986). Comprehensive coverage of "waterfront" in all aspects: context, maritime cities, river corridors, resorts, piers, marina communities, water features and water spaces.

Zeidler, Eberhard H., *Multi-Use Architecture in the Urban Context* (New York: Van Nostrand Reinhold Company, 1983).

Zunker, Vernon G., *A Dream Come True: Robert Hugman and San Antonio River Walk*, (San Antonio, Texas, 1983).

PERIODICALS

ARTICLES

Breen, Ann and Rigby, Dick, "Festival Markets —Show Stealers of the Waterfront," in *Journal of the New England Aquarium*, 1988 and *EPA Journal*, Vol.14 No.4, May 1988.

Breen, Ann and Rigby, Dick, "On the Waterfront: Revitalization from Coast to Coast," in *Planning*, Vol. 45 No. 11, November 1979.

Editorial, "Prospect—New Directions in Waterfronts, Here and Abroad," in *Landscape Architecture*, Vol. 81. No. 2, February 1991.

Various, "Theme: Docklands Challenge," in *The Architectural Review*, Vol. CLXXXI No.1080, February 1987.

PERIODICALS—THEME ISSUES

"Architecture & Water," theme issue of *A.D. Architectural Design*, London.

"La Transformación de la ciudad Puerto Madero," in *ARQUIS Arquitectura y Urbanismo*, 1994, Universidad de Palermo, Buenos Aires.

"New Urban Waterfronts," theme issue of *Landscape Architecture*, February 1991. A professional journal.

"Urban Waterfronts," theme issue of *Progressive Architecture*, June 1975. A professional journal.

"Waterfront," theme issue of *Process: Architecture*, No. 82, November 1984, Tokyo. A professional journal, illustrated.

WATERFRONT PERIODICALS

Sea History, National Maritime Historical Society, New York.

Waterfront World, The Waterfront Center, The Waterfront Press, Washington, D. C.

INFORMATION RESOURCES

ASSOCIATION INTERNATIONALE DE VILLES & PORTS

Antoine Rufenacht, president

45, rue Lord Kitchener

76600 Le Havre, France

Tel. 33 35 42 78 84 Fax 33 35 42 21 94

Oriented toward ports, the organization runs an international conference every other year in varied locations and also organizes seminars.

CATALONIAN COLLEGE OF ARCHITECTS

Ignasi Perez Arnal

Place Nova, 5

08002 Barcelona, Spain

Tel. 34 3 301 5000 Fax 34 3 412 3964

Publishes *Quaderns*, a magazine in Spanish and English that covers European architectural developments, including many waterfront projects.

CITTA D'ACQUA CENTRO INTERNAZIONALE

Rinio Bruttomesso, director

San Marco, 875

30124 Venice, Italy

Tel. 41 52 82 103 Fax 41 52 86 103

Academic in orientation, the center concerns itself with a broad range of issues affecting cites on the water, such as rising sea level and marine transport. Sponsored an international conference on waterfront developments in 1991.

INTERNATIONAL ASSOCIATION OF PORTS AND HARBORS

H. Kusaka, secretary general

Kolchira Kaikan Bldg.,1-2-8 Toranomon

Minato-ku, Tokyo 105 Japan

INTERNATIONAL MARINA INSTITUTE

Paul Dodson, director

35 Steamboat Avenue

Wickford, R.I. 02852 USA

Tel. 1 401 294 9558 Fax 1 401 294 1630

Organizes an annual marina conference and numerous specialty workshops and training courses.

TECHNOLOGY RESEARCH CENTER FOR RIVERFRONT DEVELOPMENT

Tadafumi Maejima

Ichibancho Eighty-One Building, 6th floor/6-4 Ichibancho Chiyoda-ku, Tokyo 102 Japan

URBAN & ECONOMIC DEVELOPMENT GROUP (URBED)

Nicholas Falk, director

3 Stamford Street

London SE1 9NT, UK

Tel. 44 171 928 9515 Fax 44 171 261 1015

Has produced several studies and articles on waterfront redevelopment in the UK and has conducted research elsewhere in Europe.

THE PRINCE OF WALES INSTITUTE OF ARCHITECTURE

Brian Hanson, director

14-15 Gloucester Gate, Regent's Park

London NW1 4HG, UK

Tel. 44 171 016 7380 Fax 44 171 016 7381

Publishes *Perspectives on Architecture* (address: 2 Hinde Street, London W1M 5RH, UK, tel. 44 171 224 1766, fax 44 171 224 1768), periodical with widespread coverage of architecture and urban-planning issues, principally in the UK and Europe.

THE WATERFRONT CENTER

Ann Breen and Dick Rigby, co-directors

1622 Wisconsin Avenue, N.W.

Washington, D.C. 20007 USA

Tel. 1 202 337 0356 Fax 1 202 625 1654

Formed in 1981, a non-profit educational organization that provides community consulting services, organizes the major annual international conference on urban waterfront planning, development and culture, and provides topical workshops on such subjects as aquarium/nature center planning and management. Also organizes an international awards program every year to recognize top waterfront projects, plans and volunteer citizens' efforts.

WATERFRONT REVITALIZATION RESEARCH CENTER (WARRC)

Kiyoyasu Mikanagi, president

Barque Shibaura 26-1, Kaigan 3-Chome

Minato-ku, Tokyo 108 Japan

Tel. 813 5443 5382 Fax 813 5443 5380

An affiliate of the Ministry of Transportation, this professional organization provides technical assistance to Japanese cities and towns engaged in waterfront projects. WARRC is also interested in international exchanges.

Note: *Architecture and landscape architecture associations exist in most countries and include project data in their publications. Only a few, however, simultaneously publish in English. Especially helpful architectural association libraries are listed in the Acknowledgments.*

ACKNOWLEDGMENTS

We are indebted to a great number of people who assisted in gathering material for this book. In ways large and small, they made it possible to for us to get a handle on the story.

First we thank those who gave extra time and effort on our behalf, in the chronological order that they did so: Riek Bakker of Rotterdam, a good friend, helpful in tracking down projects in Europe, host at a delightful dinner and welcome companion in Cape May; Lisa Cheng, Hong Kong, arranger of a comprehensive two-day site visit around Hong Kong and the New Territory; Keimi Harada of Tokyo, who not only organized meetings, lectures and appointments but accompanied us on many tours and enabled us to share a special evening with his family; Tsuneo Mitake of Tokyo for

escorting us, again, to Yokohama, where five years ago we saw a blank site that is now developing into one of the world's largest waterfront precincts.

We also thank Kiyoyasu Mikanagi and Tsugio Adachi of the Waterfront Revitalization Research Center, Tokyo, for making available the considerable resources of the organization and for some very pleasant social occasions; Junko Nagamuro Katoh for a wonderful reunion in Nagoya and a thorough and enjoyable tour; Carlos Mariani and Maria Perez Maraviglia, whom we met at one of our workshops on aquariums and who kindly arranged for us to visit Mar del Plata while in Argentina; Gordon Anderson, Melbourne, for arranging a thoughtful, thorough and altogether pleasant itinerary there;

Bill Norrie of Winnipeg, for a personally conducted tour of his city that only a former mayor could give; and Charlotte DeWitt, now of Stockholm, the hostess extraordinaire.

Nick Falk and Esther Caplin were generous hosts in England and exceptional tour guides, and Nick gave us wise counsel about waterfront projects throughout the UK. We are grateful to Tim Catchpole of London, a longtime associate, who also helped sort out our itinerary, and to the wonderful Coldstreams for their friendship and hospitality.

Thanks to Grania and Nick Farrow, who were jolly hosts, and to Grania, then a photo editor at Thames and Hudson, who arranged in 1993 for us to meet our publishers, who came up with the original concept for this book.

Lastly, our thanks to Katrien Prak, who was fortuitously with us in Cape May during the last days of writing, for assistance with German translations, and for good companionship.

We thank the Sir Herbert Manzoni Scholarship Trust of Birmingham, UK, for again supporting our work. We are also grateful for the generous financial assistance of K. Bailey, Boulder, Colorado; John Belle, New York City; C. Chang, Oakland, California; J. J. C. van Rijs, Maliebaan, The Netherlands; John and Judy Lentz, Bethesda, Maryland; Makers Architecture and Urban Design, Seattle, Washington; Leo Molinaro, Columbia, Maryland; Potomac Riverboat Co., Alexandria, Virginia; Realvest Corp., Vancouver, Washington; Leighton Taylor, St. Helena, California; Yolanda Velez, Mayagüez, Puerto Rico, and Paul Willen, Chappaqua, New York.

We appreciate the efforts of a number of librarians, including Fien Veltman, Netherlands Architecture Institute, Rotterdam; Susan Day, Institut Français d'Architecture, Paris; Edda Riese, Humboldt-Bibliothek, Tegel, Berlin; Frid Welde, Det Norske Arkiteketakademi Biblioteket, Oslo; Valerie Tring, Sydney Opera House Library; Hugh Whitman, Loeb Library, Harvard Graduate School of Design, Cambridge, Massachusetts, and most especially, Carole Twombly, American Institute of Architects Library, Washington, D.C.

We are further indebted to a number of professional photographers who kindly gave us permission to use their work on these pages. They are: Inken Kuntze, Shigeo Ogawa, Tomio Ohashi, Steve Rosenthal and Peter Vanderwarker.

We list here, by city, those who further assisted, some on site, others by mail and fax. In many cases, the person listed is the one actually transmitting information and/or photos while principals are listed with the project. Apologies to anyone we somehow overlook.

Amalfi Marta Moretti (Venice)
Amsterdam Leon Thier, Ton Schaap
Aomori Harushige Takeuchi
Antwerp Pierre Tack, bOb Van Reeth
Auckland Ian Batcheldor, Stewart Kendon
Baltimore David Benn
Barcelona Diana Garrigosa i Laspenas, Enrique Caldentey, Marta Flo, Jean-Pierre Lutz, Jaume Mach, Gabriel Bora, Robert Terradas Muntanola, Rafael Caceres, Sergio Brosa del Pozo, Mark Smith
Bergen Oivind Maurseth
Berlin Mark Denton, Asha Moorthy (Santa Monica, California)
Boston Lorraine Downey, Charles and Diane Norris, Elizabeth Stembler
Birmingham, UK Tom Brock (Tamworth)
Brisbane Bruce Derrick
Bristol Sara Bailey, Hugh Stebbing, Tim Martienssen
Buenos Aires Raul Cohen, Gonzalo W. P. Bunge

Cape Town David Jack, Michael Carney
Cardiff Neil M. C. Sinclair, Hank Haff (Cambridge, Massachusetts)
Charleston, South Carolina Stuart Dawson (Watertown, Massachusetts)
Chicago Jane Thompson (Cambridge, Massachusetts)
Duluth, Minnesota Gerald Kimball
Dundee Gillian Menmuir
Düsseldorf Manuela Papakakis (Frankfurt)
Exeter John Clark
Fort Lauderdale, Florida Douglas Coolman, Martha Lord
Genova Elena Kazias and Fred Wales (Cambridge, Massachusetts)
Gloucester, UK Alyson Sheppard
Gold Coast Elisabeth Kumm
Grimsby Kevin Withers, Paul Rayton and Clive Nicholson (Cambridge, UK)
Groningen Frans Haks
Haifa Zvi Miller, Yigal Tzamir
Hamburg Elisabeth von Renner, Tony Schroter, Bernd Pastuschka (also for Lübeck), Lizzie Nelstrop (London)
Hakodate Masaji Abe
Halifax Fred Were, Linda Gourlay
Helsinki Teresia Liljelund, Heikki Hirvonen
Hiroshima Prof. Nobuaki Furuya (Tokyo)
Hobart Elizabeth Fowler, Barry Shelton and Bruce Churchill
Hong Kong Brian Wong, Lau Kwok-Choi, Frances K. F. Lam, Keit Tan and Ms. Anita Leung
Hull S. Goodhand
Husum Prof. Berhnard Winking
Kobe Akio Tsuji, Toyoko Matsumoto and Koichi Ikemoto
Köln Ingrid Kolb, Claudia Kader
Kuching William Morrison (Sydney)
Kushiro Yutaka Matsubara (Tokyo)
Leeds Len Davies, Jonathan Wix
Liverpool Tony Lynch
London Mark Freeman and Rachel Escott, A. D. Smerdon and John Outram
Louvain-la-Neuve Yoshiko Takanmawa (Tokyo)
Lowell, Massachusetts Chris Briggs
Lübeck Evita von Zitzewitz
Macao Lorenzo and Filomena Vicente
Manchester Claire Onslow
Marseille Eric Castaldi, Erick Zerbib
Melbourne Bill Chandler, John Noonan, Douglas Daines and David Cole
Mexico City Mario Schjetnan
Mikkeli Arto Sipinen
Monterey, California Chuck Davis (San Francisco)
Nagoya Tsuyosi Takagi
Nanao Tadashi Miyazaki
Newcastle Gwendolyn and Stephen Harbottle, Carole Carr

Norrköping Arne Ellefors, Kaj Krantz and Thorbjorn Andersson (Stockholm)
Oakland, California Rick Wiederhorn, Frank Dobson
Osaka Atsushi Semba, Takayuki Tokuhira, Irie Shingo, Nobukatsu Shima, Koji Morita, Shigeo Iida, Kuzuhiro Nose, Isao Osumi, Reiko Fukushima, Mark Brady, Akira Nisio and Yumiko Oka; also Lyn Hogan (San Francisco), Peter Chermayeff (Cambridge, Massachusetts)
Oslo Neils Torp, Pal Moen and Kari Nissen Brodtkorb
Palma Ramon Felix
Paris Julia Fainsilber (also Strasbourg), Bernard Tschumi (New York)
Pittsburgh Arthur Zeigler and Albert Tannier
Portland, Oregon Robert Murase
Providence, Rhode Island William Warner and David Brussat
Riga Ilze Jones (Seattle)
San Antonio Richard Hurd
San Juan Victor Negrón, Joan Bloom (New York)
Santos Marilia Rossi Nogueira, Doris Sloan (San Francisco)
Singaporo Mrs. Cheong Koon Hean, Mrs. Teh Lai Yip, Miss Waheeda Abdul Rahim, Ms. Hwang Yu-Ning and Lyn Hogan (San Francisco)
Stockholm Ann Charlotte Englund and the National Maritime Historical Society (Peekskill, New York)
Stockton-on-Tees Cindy Hadcand
Strahan, Tasmania Grant and Ilze Jones, Bill Mabey
Sunderland Lucy Milton
Swansea David M. Wilson
Sydney Susan and Barry Young, Terry Jones, Di Talty, Penelope Coombs, Susan Duyker and Janet Roderick
Toronto, Ontario Eberhard Zeidler
Tokyo Hajime Owada, Tsuneo Yamauchi, Syojiro Ishikura, Nobuaki Furuya, Kiyonori Kikutake, Nobuyoshi Takagi, Hideo Kayahara, Hirofumi Teranishi, Yutaka Matsubara, Tomoo Ishiwata, Kenichi Ogawa, Masatoshi Mitsutomi, Toshimitsu Nishiyama, Yasuyuki Nakayama, Hiroshi Matsumnoto, Oguama Hiroyuki, Mitsukuni Tsuchiya, Ryosuke Komine, Masakatsu Honma, Tashimitsu Mishiyama, Kunihiko Matsumoto and Yasuo Takahashi
Venice Antonio DiMambro (Boston, Massachusetts)
Whangarei Ron Esveld
Winnipeg, Manitoba Doug Clark, Mayor Susan Thompson
Yokohama Hitoshi Wada, Tetsuya Makajhima and Yoshiki Osada, Goro Fukumori, Ikuo Muto (Tokyo), Ikuko Akiyoshi and Nachinko Kudo (New York)

By no means last in effort are our associates at the Waterfront Center, namely Ginny Murphy, Susan Kirk and Jackie Conn, who held the enterprise together for two years while we concentrated on this book. Also, Christina Van Ness of California, who, using her native German,

221

volunteered to unlock doors in that country. Martha Gil Montero, a good friend and guide to things Latin American, and a fellow author, provided us with good contacts and helped with liaison and translation tasks.

We were blessed with two young women who put in many hours on this project. Jennifer Bartlett wrote us about how much she enjoyed our first book and volunteered her services to the Waterfront Center. We set her about tracking projects, which she did admirably, overcoming more than a few hurdles. We wish her well in her career as a planner.

In 1994, Kaija Jones of Seattle stayed with Ann while doing an internship in Washington, D.C. Following that, she gradually became a fixture at the Waterfront Center, diligently pursuing project information around the globe for this book in the last months of the effort. Her assistance in the final push was crucial.

A.B./D.R.

ILLUSTRATION SOURCES

The illustrations used in these pages are reproduced with the permission of the following (abbreviations used: A, above; B, below; C, center; L, left; M, middle; R, right; T, top):

2–3: Wolfgang Burat **6** top row: L, Port of Nagoya (Port of Nagoya, Japan); CL, Ian Cave (Leeds Waterfront, UK); CR, (South Horizons, Hong Kong) R, Brian Gilkes (Southbank, Melbourne, Australia); 2nd row: L, © Simon Scott/Thom Bing, Architect (False Creek Yacht Club, Vancouver, Canada); C, City of Rotterdam (White House building, Rotterdam, The Netherlands); R, John Gollings (Bond University, Gold Coast, Australia); 3rd row: L, Courtesy of TGP Landschaftsarchitekten (Musik- und Kongresshalle, Lübeck, Germany); bottom row: L, Patrick Bingham-Hall (Exhibition Centre, Darling Harbour, Sydney, Australia); R, John Outram (Storm Water Pumping Station, London, UK); **7** top row: C, Minneapolis Dept. of Recreation (Lake Harriet Bandshell, Minneapolis, Minnesota, USA); R, (detail from museum/library, Puerto Real, Cádiz, Spain); 2nd row C, James Higgins (Lowell, Massachusetts historic park, USA); R, Breen/Rigby (pedestrian bridge leading from port building to aquarium, Port of Nagoya, Japan); 3rd row: MC, © Heiner Leiska (Elbschlucht office and restaurant building, Hamburg, Germany); 4th row: L, (Hay's Galleria, London, UK); R, Northern Publishing (boating center, Whangarei, New Zealand); bottom: L, Takeshiba Pier Redevelopment (Takeshiba Pier, Tokyo, Japan); R, Breen/Rigby (Swansea Maritime Quarter, Wales, UK) **10**: Breen/Rigby; **11**: Perkins & Will **12**: Breen/Rigby **13**: A, Breen/Rigby; B, Edward D. Stone, Jr. & Assoc. **14–17**: Breen/Rigby **18**: Sabine Schneiders Luftbilder **19**: Breen/Rigby **20**: Judy K. Jacobsen **21**: Sasaki Associates **22**: Louisville Waterfront Development Corp./Vincent C. Re **23**: Breen/Rigby **24**: M. E. Warren **26**: A, B, Nikken Sekkei/Karoku Kato **27**: A, Port of Yokohama; M, Nikken Sekkei/Karoku Kato; BL, Breen/Rigby **28**: A, ML, Breen/Rigby; **28–9**: Nikken Sekkei/Karoku Kato **30**: T, ML, Nikken Sekkei/ Karoku Kato; MR, BL, Breen/Rigby **31**: Nikken Sekkei/Karoku Kato **32–3**: William D. Warner Architects, Ltd. **34**: A, Bryggedrift A/S; B, Breen/Rigby **35**: A, Bengston, Solvang, Winsnes/Telje-Torp-Aasen; B, Telje-Torp-Aasen **36** Telje-Torp-Aasen **37**: Bengston, Solvang, Winsnes/Telje-Torp-Aasen **38**: A, B, Breen/Rigby; M, Telje-Torp-Aasen **39**: AL, B, Kari Nissen Brodtkorb; AR, Breen/Rigby **40–1**: Darling Harbour Authority/MSJ Keys Young **42**: AL, Breen/Rigby; M, Darling Harbour Authority; BL, MSJ Keys Young **44**: Nikken

Sekkei/ATC Photo **45**: ATC EDAW, 1995 **46**: L, BL, Port and Harbor Bureau City of Osaka/Mark Brady; R, Nikken Sekkei **47**: Nikken Sekkei **48–51**: Tyne & Wear Development Corp. **52–3**: Courtesy Birmingham City Council, Dept. of Planning **54–5**: Birmingham Dept. of Planning and Architecture **56**: © Photo Library Mark Van Aardt **57**: ML, BL, © Photo Library Mark Van Aardt; AR, BR, Victoria and Alfred Waterfront **58**: © Heiner Leiska **60**: Skidmore, Owings & Merrill **61**: The Beacon Companies **62**: © Peter Vanderwarker **63**: AR, © Peter Vanderwarker; L, BR, Skidmore, Owings and Merrill **64–5**: © 1987 Steve Rosenthal **66**: A, GGLO Architecture and Interior Design; B, City of Portland Development Commission **67**: A, Alain Grainger; B, City of Portland Development Commission **68–73**: Brian Gilkes Photography **74–9**: bOb Van Reeth **80**: Fiona Spalding-Smith/Zeidler Roberts Partnership, Architects **81–2**: Zeidler Roberts Partnership, Architects **83**: Richard Bryant/Arcaid/Zeidler Roberts Partnership, Architects **83**: Fiona Spalding-Smith/Zeidler Roberts Partnership, Architects **84–6**: Jason Springer **87**: Jane Thompson **88**: Inken Kuntze **90**: Osaka Waterfront Development Co. Ltd./Cambridge Seven Associates **91**: Y. Matsmura **92–3**: Monterey Bay Aquarium **94–6**: Photo Tomio Ohashi/Tadao Ando Architect **97**: ML, BR, BL, Photo Tomio Ohashi/Tadao Ando Architect; AL, AR, Shinkenchiku-sha/Tadao Ando Architect **98–103**: Grupo de Diseño Urbano, S.C. **104–7**: Arto Kiviniemi **108–9**: John Stoel **110–11**: Breen/Rigby **112**: Sydney Opera House Trust; Don McMurdo/Peter Garrett Photographers **113**: AL, AR, Breen/Rigby; BR, Sydney Opera House Trust; Don McMurdo/Peter Garrett Photographers **114**: James Higgins **116**: A, Cohlmeyer Hanson and Associates, Winnipeg; B, City of Winnipeg **117**: AR, Cohlmeyer Hanson and Associates, Winnipeg; BL, BR, City of Winnipeg **118–21**: Eric Castaldi **122–5**: Urban Redevelopment Authority, Singapore **126**: Breen/Rigby **127**: Bengt Pettersson **128**: Breen/Rigby **129**: Breen/Rigby **130–1**: Corporación Antiguo Puerto Madero **132**: Derek Ross **133**: AR, BR, Simon Kenny; MC, Sydney Cove Authority **134–5**: Derek Ross **136**: Teeside Development Corp. **138–9**: Breen/Rigby **140**: Tokyo Metropolitan Government **141**: Breen/Rigby **142**: P. Astiev/Adrien Fainsilber Architecte **143**: P. Hurlin/Adrien Fainsilber Architecte **144–5**: Adrien Fainsilber Architecte **146**: TR, BL, Ginny Murphy; AL, A. Fainsilber; MR, Bernard Tschumi **147**: AL, MR, Ginny Murphy; BR, S. Couturier/Adrien Fainsilber Architecte **148**: Conybeare Morrison and Partners **149**:

William Morrison **150–1**: John Gollings **152**: © Peter Vanderwarker **154**: Atelier PRO Architekten **155–7**: Peter de Rug **158–9**: Ger van der Vlugt/Atelier PRO Architekten **162–3**: PLAN, Moore Ruble Yudell **160–3**: Timothey Hursley **164–7**: Heiner Leiska **168**: Julkaistavaan Kuvaan on Merkittava **169**: AL, AR, Breen/Rigby; B, Helsinki City Planning Department **170**: © Peter Vanderwarker **172**: Minoru Takeyama **173**: AL, BR, Minoru Takeyama; AR, BL, Bureau of Port and Harbor, Tokyo Metropolitan Government **174**: Minoru Takeyma **175**: Bureau of Port and Harbor, Tokyo Metropolitan Government **176**: AL, AR, Breen/Rigby; B, Minoru Takeyama **177**: Bureau of Port and Harbor, Tokyo Metropolitan Government **178**: Port of Oakland/Jordan Woodman Dobson **179**: Jordan Woodman Dobson **180**: AR, Jordan Woodman Dobson; BL, BR, Port of Oakland/Jordan Woodman Dobson **181**: Port of Oakland/Jordan Woodman Dobson **182**: R, Tom Paive/Jordan Woodman Dobson; L, Port of Oakland/Jordan Woodman Dobson **183**: Port of Oakland/Jordan Woodman Dobson **184–7**: Alsop + Störmer **188**: L, Baltimore Development Corp./Rouse Co. **189**: L, Bill Murton; R, City of Duluth **190**: L, Edward D. Stone, Jr. and Associates; R, The Armour Group/Waterfront Development Corp. **191**: C, Mariani Perez Maraviglia; R, Steve Rosenthal/Benjamin Thompson & Associates **193**: Pittsburgh History and Landmarks Foundation **194**: L, Bob Krist for the Puerto Rico Tourism Co.; R, Port of Seattle **195**: L, Fred Housel; M, Canada Place Architects/Downs Archambault Musson/Cattel & Partners/Zeidler Roberts Partnership **196**: L, Port of Aomori; C, Breen/Rigby **197**: L, Port of Hakodate; R, Courtesy of Regional Services Dept., Hong Kong **198**: L, Hsin-Yieh Architects & Associates, Ltd.; C, Courtesy of Regional Council, Hong Kong; R, Port and Harbor Bureau, City of Kobe **200**: L, Courtesy of Sasaki Associates R, Nanao Fisherman's Wharf **201**: Takeshiba Pier Redevelopment **202**: Mitsubishi Estate Co., Ltd. **203**: L, Challenge Properties; R, John Gollings **204**: David Moore **205**: Arnolfini **206**: L, J.J. Photographic; C, Leon/Arazola **207**: Spanphoto **208**: John Clark, Exeter City Council **209**: L, Italimpianti Photo; C, Pearce Developments Ltd.; R, Courtesy of Great Grimsby Borough Council **210**: Hull Museum of Transportation **211**: R. Barten **213**: Hay's Galleria **214**: L, Courtesy of TGP Landschaftsarchitekten; C, Breen/Rigby **215**: José Antonio Martinez Lapena/Elias Torres Tur **216**: Breen/Rigby **217**: Colin Wilbourn

INDEX

Featured projects in **bold**, Gazetteer entries in *italic*